MAN OF THE YEAR

A TIME Honored Tradition

FIFTEEN CENTS

January 2, 1928

TIME

The Weekly Newsmagazine

Charles A. Lindbergh
May 27, 1927

THE MAN OF THE YEAR
He defeated fame.
(See HEROES)

Volume XI

Number 1

Publication and Circulation Offices, Penton Building, Cleveland. Editorial and Advertising Offices, 25 West 45th Street, New York.

MAN OF THE YEAR

A TIME Honored Tradition

Frederick S. Voss
National Portrait Gallery

NPG
TWENTY-FIFTH
ANNIVERSARY
1962-1987

Smithsonian Institution Press
Washington, D.C.   London

Library of Congress Cataloging-in-Publication Data

Voss, Frederick.
  Man of the year.

  Bibliography: p.
  1. Man of the year selections—Exhibitions.
2. Biography—20th century—Portraits—Exhibitions.
3. Celebrities—Portraits—Exhibitions. 4. Magazine
covers—United States—Exhibitions. 5. National Portrait
Gallery (Smithsonian Institution)—Exhibitions.
I. Time, the weekly news-magazine. II. Title.
CT120.V67   1987   757'.9'09730740153   87-12877
ISBN 0-87474-949-2 (alk. paper)

∞ The paper used in this publication meets the minimum
requirements of the American National Standard for
Permanence of Paper for Printed Library
Materials   Z39.48-1984.

National Portrait Gallery
Alan Fern, Director
Beverly J. Cox, Curator of Exhibitions
Suzanne C. Jenkins, Registrar
Nello Marconi, Chief, Design and Production
Frances Kellogg Stevenson, Publications Officer

Cover illustration:
Winston Churchill, named by *TIME* as Man of the Half-Century in 1949.
National Portrait Gallery, Smithsonian Institution; Gift of Time, Inc.

Frontispiece:
TIME cover of Charles Lindbergh, January 2, 1928; original art by Samuel
Johnson Woolf (1880–1948)

Contents

Foreword

The collection of covers from TIME Magazine is a very special part of the National Portrait Gallery. Normally, the Gallery looks back into history, and tries to determine who made notable contributions in the many fields of endeavor that constitute the society and culture of the United States of America. When life portraits of these men and women in painting, sculpture, prints, and photographs can be located, they are acquired for the museum's permanent collection after individual consideration by staff curators and historians, and deliberation by the Gallery's Commissioners on the historical significance of the sitter and quality of the portrayal.

In contrast, the *TIME* covers are records of the present day. They are accepted precisely because they were chosen as featured portraits on the magazine, and thereby constitute a record of the people regarded by the editors as noteworthy that week. It is inevitable that some of those accorded a cover on *TIME* will fade into obscurity in the decades to come, but for the most part the track record of the editors has been prescient. Many of the portraits of the most significant twentieth-century political, scientific, and cultural leaders at the National Portrait Gallery are found in the TIME collection, and without question many more are yet to come.

Starting in 1927, *TIME*'s editors began a new approach to the first cover of the new year. In microcosm, they began a process not unlike what is done at the Gallery in selecting subjects for our collection. The Gallery looks back as far as American history stretches, but *TIME* reviews the year just past and selects the person (or sometimes the people) who made the greatest impact on the world during that period. For this publication, and the exhibition upon which it has been based, Gallery historian Frederick Voss has made a selection of "Men (and women, and topics) of the Year" that provides a unique opportunity to reflect on the course of the past sixty years, and to recall people and phenomena that most shaped the period. Unlike the weekly cover choices, these subjects are almost always of enduring fame, and, since *TIME* is an American publication, even those who are not Americans by nationality have by definition left their mark on the United States.

The *TIME* collection has been of enormous benefit to the Gallery in another way: it has brought the work of a number of prominent contemporary artists into the museum. At first the Man of the Year portraits were done by the illustrators who worked regularly for *TIME*, but starting in the 1960s the weekly often turned to painters and sculptors of international reputation to do this most important of its covers. Thus—along with images by some of *TIME*'s most frequent cover makers, such as S. J. Woolf, Ernest Hamlin Baker, and Boris Artzybasheff—this volume includes works by Alfred Leslie, Marisol, and Peter Hurd. In addition, *TIME* commissioned covers (not included here) from such people as Philip Pearlstein, Alice Neel, and Frank Gallo, among others.

As originally presented to the public, reproduced on the magazine's pages of uniform size, the quality and diversity of style found in the Man of the Year images is not nearly as evident as when the originals themselves are viewed. By reproducing them here from the original paintings, drawings, and sculpture, we hope that we have suggested how powerful some of these pieces can be as works of art in their own right, in addition to their effectiveness for their original purpose.

Each year the Gallery selects a group of covers from TIME for display in a room devoted to the collection. Usually these are drawn from the originals given to the Gallery by Time, Inc. But this selection, devoted as it is to a special kind of cover, has drawn as well from originals that for one reason or another had found their way back to the artist or into another public collection. We are grateful to the owners of these works for allowing us to augment our own holdings by making available the portraits they possessed. With their cooperation, we are able to tell a particularly interesting part of the *TIME*-cover story, and to recall a number of personalities notable in our recent history.

Alan Fern
Director
National Portrait Gallery

Acknowledgments

This publication, and the Man of the Year exhibition that inspired it, grew out of the efforts and goodwill of many. Among the parties to whom a special vote of thanks is owing are the four institutions—Syracuse University, the Germantown Friends School of Philadelphia, the New York Public Library, and the George C. Marshall Research Foundation—which consented to the use of their Man of the Year portraits both here and in the exhibition. We are also immensely grateful to the late Muriel Woolf Hobson who, when asked to lend her 1938 Man of the Year portrait of Madame and General Chiang Kai-shek by her father, S. J. Woolf, instead presented it to the National Portrait Gallery as a gift. Also indispensable to this enterprise have been many members of the Gallery's own staff, including its able photographers Gene Mantie and Rolland White and its editors Frances Stevenson and Dru Dowdy.

But nothing would have been possible without Time, Inc., which in 1978 presented this museum with more than eight-hundred pieces of original *TIME* cover artwork, and has made three similar gifts since then. Our gratitude for this generosity is, therefore, substantial indeed on this occasion, for it is from among this body of twentieth-century images that most of the pieces reproduced here were drawn. To Time, Inc., a debt of thanks is also owing for its willingness to defray part of the expenses for publishing this book, and we at the same time offer our profound appreciation to *TIME*'s art director, Rudy Hoglund, and his deputy, Dorothy Chapman, for all of their assistance and encouragement in this undertaking.

Introduction

On the evening of May 17, 1963, Vice-President Lyndon B. Johnson was belatedly entering New York's Waldorf Astoria to attend a dinner marking the fortieth anniversary of *TIME* magazine. In its four decades of existence, *TIME* had risen from a shoestring enterprise, which most veterans of publishing thought would surely die aborning, to the most widely circulated newsweekly in America. In the process, its red-bordered portrait covers—depicting the most newsworthy luminaries of the moment—had become a ubiquitous feature on the nation's reading tables and newsstands. Understandably there was much pride felt in this accomplishment, and, to usher in the magazine's fifth decade of publication, its founder, Henry Luce, had convened at the Waldorf 284 of the notables who had appeared over the years on its cover. The late-arriving Johnson had by then held that most coveted of spots three times. When he stepped onto the speaker's dais to deliver some brief remarks, he began by noting that many of those present—including himself—"owe Harry Luce a very great debt" for his policy of making cover selections "on a basis other than beauty."[1]

Indeed, when Henry Luce and his cofounder, Briton Hadden, were planning the maiden issue of *TIME* in the early months of 1923, it never occurred to them that fine chins or good bone structure should have anything to do with their choice of cover subject. According to their new enterprise's prospectus, they intended to report news in terms of the personalities who shaped it.[2] They knew, of course, that if their covers were to reflect this bias toward individuals, it followed that achievement, and not beauty, would be the primary factor in determining who would appear on their covers. Thus the person gracing the cover of *TIME*'s first issue on March 3, 1923, was not an alluring starlet of the silent screen; instead it was the gaunt, eighty-six-year-old "Uncle Joe" Cannon [Fig. 1] who, after forty years of wielding power in the House of Representatives, had announced his retirement from public life.

So the pattern was set. As the new magazine struggled for survival and then passed into prosperity, week after week, year in and year out, its subscribers could expect to find below the boldly lettered *TIME* logo a drawn, painted, or photographic likeness of a current newsmaker. By the early 1930s the magazine's almost-always-predictable cover-portrait format was becoming as much of a journalistic institution as its distinctively colorful and sometimes irreverent prose.

Beyond the rationale implied in *TIME*'s original prospectus, Hadden and Luce never offered an explanation for what prompted their determination to make portraits the primary subject matter of their covers. In the absence of any such statement, it is perhaps dangerous to probe the matter much further. Nevertheless, it is worth speculating that, in part at least, the magazine's cover likenesses were almost certainly emblematic of a fundamental faith that individual talent and creativity can and do make a crucial difference in this world. This may not seem particularly significant until we consider the present day, where technology, bureaucracy, and corporate power often appear to have displaced people as the shapers of events. In that light, *TIME*'s portrait tradition invites reflection on the

Figure 1. *TIME* cover of Joseph Cannon, March 3, 1923
Original art by William Oberhardt (1882–1950)

Figure 2. *John L. Lewis* 1880–1969
By Samuel J. Woolf (1880–1948)
Charcoal and chalk on paper, 32.8 x 27 cm. (12 15/16 x 10 5/8 in.), 1933
TIME cover, October 2, 1933
National Portrait Gallery, Smithsonian Institution; gift of Time, Inc.

Figure 3. *Oveta Culp Hobby* born 1905

By Ernest Hamlin Baker (1889–1975)
Watercolor on paper, 33.4 x 30.5 cm.
    (13 3/16 x 12 in.), 1944
TIME cover, January 17, 1944
National Portrait Gallery, Smithsonian
    Institution; gift of Oveta Culp Hobby

Figure 4. *Maria Callas* 1923–1977 (detail)

By Henry Koerner (born 1915)
Oil on canvas, 55.9 x 71.1 cm. (22 x 28 in.),
    1956
TIME cover, October 29, 1956
National Portrait Gallery, Smithsonian
    Institution; gift of Time, Inc.

contrast between the human condition as it was interpreted in 1923 and as it is commonly perceived today, even on the covers of *TIME*.

During its first forty years of publication *TIME* featured a good many photographic likenesses on its covers, but its trademark image—the one that most Americans conjured up in their minds at mention of the magazine's name—was a drawn or painted portrait. Over time, the prevailing look of these non-photographic renderings changed. Through the 1920s and much of the 1930s, for example, the cover most typically featured an image originally drawn in charcoal [Fig. 2]. By World War II, these black-and-white drawings had been displaced by immaculately detailed painted portraits in watercolor, gouache, or tempera [Fig. 3]. By the mid-1950s this sharp, journalistic fidelity to the subject had begun to alternate with likenesses of a more broadly painted and somewhat less literal sort [Fig. 4]. In general, however, the always-changing stable of artists, who supplied *TIME* with its covers through the early 1960s, by and large leaned to a traditional realism in their portraiture.

Beginning in about 1965, however, the magazine's cover portraits became increasingly less predictable, and the types of images seen on the cover expanded enormously. In 1967, when Bob Hope was slated for the cover, the editors turned to the modernist sculptor Marisol (Escobar) to do a semiabstract rendering of America's favorite comedian [Fig. 5]. By then, the magazine had also begun to employ caricature, and when political writer William Buckley appeared on the cover in 1967, he found himself trenchantly depicted by David Levine as a kind of anthropomorphized beaver [Fig. 6]. For Robert F. Kennedy's portrait of 1966 *TIME* ventured into the avant-garde world of pop art and commissioned Roy Lichtenstein to depict the New York senator as comic-strip superman [Fig. 7].[3]

But, however far afield *TIME* went in its portraiture, one tradition—dating from its fourth year of publication—remained intact. As sure as winter followed fall and Christmas Thanksgiving, subscribers to *TIME* could always be sure that the cover image on the magazine's first issue of every year would depict the person or persons who "for better or for worse" had most dominated events in the previous twelve months.

Like many annual rituals, the designation of a man of the year every January came about through an accidental combination of circumstances that only later were seen as a blessing. The year was 1927; it was the last week in December; and, due doubtless to the holiday season, the normal flow of public events had temporarily ebbed to a trickle. Looking to 1928, the editors at *TIME* were consequently feeling more hard-pressed than usual in arriving at a newsworthy cover subject for its first issue of the new year. At the same time, the magazine's staff were well aware that they had passed up many opportunities in the previous year to put aviator Charles Lindbergh on its cover. Ever since late May, when he had become the first man to fly nonstop from New York to Paris, the shy, sandy-haired Lindbergh had been the recipient of an unprecedented adulation from a public who clearly could not get enough of him. In the past seven months, however, *TIME* had somehow failed to note that "Lucky Lindy's" phenomenal celebrity made him an eminently ripe subject for its cover.

So, facing a dearth of other cover possibilities and wishing to make up for their earlier journalistic myopia, the editors in desperation came up with a new concept. Instead of highlighting a personality of the week, it was decided that the cover for January 2, 1928, should feature Lindbergh and that beneath his likeness would be the words "Man of the Year" [Fig. 8].[4]

Of course, the naming of such a remarkable phenomenon as Lindbergh as Man of the Year did not necessarily mean that a new annual tradition had been born. But, when the cover for *TIME*'s first issue of 1929 revealed that its editors had named car magnate Walter P. Chrysler as Man of the Year for 1928, and when, a year later, subscribers found that General Electric's board chairman, Owen Young, had earned a similar designation for 1929, it was evident that the Man of the Year was here to stay. By the mid-1930s it was also apparent that the readers of *TIME* were beginning to think that they should have a part in selecting the recipient of this annual honor. Thus, in response to *TIME*'s invitation to submit their Man of the Year preferences for 1934, a good number of readers sent in their nominations. While several thought that Louisiana's haranguing Senator Huey Long was the logical candidate, another supported first lady Eleanor Roosevelt. In the end, it was Mrs. Roosevelt's husband who, for the second time in three years, occupied what was now *TIME*'s most prestigious cover.[5]

At the same time, readers were becoming increasingly inclined to offer thoughts on the wisdom of *TIME*'s Man of the Year choice after the fact. When the magazine tapped the American divorcée Wallis Simpson [Fig. 9] as the first female Man of the Year in 1936, subscribers, by a margin of two to one, were outraged. The main distinction of the stylish Mrs. Simpson was that she had captured the heart of English monarch Edward VIII, who, in the face of unbending opposition to his marrying her, decided to abdicate his throne. Newsworthy as that was, it did not strike many *TIME* readers as sufficient reason for making her the first cover subject of 1937. "Phooey, Scallions, and Fishcakes on your most lousy choice of 'person of the year,'" fumed one. "For your editors a big and mighty Bronx cheer." To yet another—obviously troubled by the fact that Mrs. Simpson's affair with the King had begun while she was still wed to her second husband—the selection represented a "lousy insult to every faithful wife and mother in the U.S." Interestingly enough, in the final tally of reader nominations that year, Wallis Simpson had, with ex-King Edward and Franklin Roosevelt, numbered among the three most favored choices.[6] Clearly the subscribers who wished to exert influence on the choice itself and those who preferred to comment on it after it was made, in many cases, marched to very different drummers.

The Man of the Year reader plebiscites have inspired nominations over the years that have ranged everywhere from the sensible to the eccentric. While the choice of at least a handful of subscribers—and sometimes many more than that—has almost always coincided with the magazine's own ultimate judgment in the matter, some reader recommendations have been played largely for laughs. That doubtless was the case in 1963, when one reader cast his vote for the "pop top beer can" and,

Figure 5. *Bob Hope* born 1903

By Marisol (Escobar) (born 1915)
Polychromed wood, 48.2 x 38.1 x 40.6 cm.
  (19 x 15 x 16 in.), 1967
TIME cover, December 22, 1967
National Portrait Gallery, Smithsonian
  Institution; gift of Time, Inc.

Figure 6. *William F. Buckley, Jr.* born 1925

By David Levine (born 1926)
Ink on paper, 34.6 x 27.9 cm. (13 5/8 x 11
  in.), 1967
TIME cover, November 3, 1967
National Portrait Gallery, Smithsonian
  Institution; gift of Time, Inc.

Figure 7. *Robert F. Kennedy* 1925–1968

By Roy Lichtenstein (born 1923)

Silkscreen on plexiglas, 58.4 x 41.9 cm. (23
x 16 1/2 in.), 1968

TIME cover, May 24, 1968

National Portrait Gallery, Smithsonian
Institution; gift of Time, Inc.

Figure 8. *TIME* cover of Charles Lindbergh,
January 2, 1928

Original art by Samuel Johnson Woolf
(1880–1948)

nine years later, when another threw his support to that most popular fictional character of the moment, Jonathan Livingston Seagull.[7] There was also one instance when a few readers urged that the most obvious choice for Man of the Year be denied that distinction. The personage in question was Germany's Adolf Hitler, whose annexation of Austria and success several months later in claiming Czechoslovakia's Sudetenland had made his selection as 1938's Man of the Year a foregone conclusion. Foregone or not, some dreaded this choice, fearing that it would imply American acquiescence to Hitler's anti-Semitism and lust for "Lebensraum." So it was, in the last days of 1938, that *TIME* received a telegram imploring its editors to refrain from the inevitable.[8] Among the signers of this communication were movie actor Melvyn Douglas and comedian Groucho Marx, but even luminaries such as they could not keep the German Führer off *TIME*'s first cover of 1939. Nevertheless, the cable did make a point, albeit indirectly: In the past decade, the Man of the Year tradition had become a ritual in which many Americans had come to set great store.

For a long time, the cover portrayals of the Man of the Year were done by the artist-illustrators who were normally enlisted to do *TIME*'s other covers. By the early 1960s, however, the magazine had begun increasingly to view the Man of the Year image as something that ought to be treated as a special commission. In 1961 the magazine brought the internationally respected Pietro Annigoni all the way from Italy to paint John F. Kennedy at the White House. Three years later it asked the noted Southwest artist Peter Hurd and his wife, Henriette Wyeth, to go to Washington to collaborate on a likeness of Lyndon B. Johnson. When it was decided that Henry Kissinger and Richard Nixon would share the Man of the Year honors for 1972, *TIME*'s editors enlisted Marisol to carve their features in a style echoing Mount Rushmore. In the wake of these special commissionings came a new dimension to the Man of the Year tradition. In addition to Monday-morning quarterback comments on the wisdom of the Man of the Year choice itself, subscribers also began to send in critiques on the aptness of the cover image. Often the portrait proved to be nearly as controversial as the actual Man of the Year himself and sometimes more so. In fact the record for comments—both pro and con—on any *TIME* cover portrait was set by Annigoni's 1961 portrait of President Kennedy.

In the ceremony of papal investiture, there comes a point when the words "Sic transit gloria mundi" (So passes the glory of the world) are spoken over burning flax. The intent of this rite, of course, is to underscore the often-transient nature of personal power and fame in a changing world. Testing the validity of this thought against *TIME*'s Man of the Year choices in the past six decades, it is apparent that it does, indeed, hold a grain of truth. Who but a few specialized students of recent American history, for example, can recall the reasons behind General Hugh Johnson's Man of the Year designation in 1934 [Fig. 10]? At the time, the name of this burly, tough-talking chief of Franklin Roosevelt's National Recovery Administration was a widely revered household word.

But in less than a year—thanks largely to his own abrasiveness—Johnson's once-ascendant influence had reached zero point, and he was rapidly falling into an obscurity out of which he never arose. Closer to our own day, there is the case of Judge John Sirica, whose actions on the bench during the Watergate scandals paved the way for a President's resignation and earned Sirica himself a place on one of *TIME*'s Man of the Year covers. Americans over thirty may think that Sirica's name will never be forgotten, but they should know that there are many entering adulthood at this moment who are no more than vaguely aware—if at all—of the pivotal role this Federal jurist played in one of the most earthshaking political events of the near past.

This is not to suggest that many of the Man of the Year selections proved in the long term to be trivial. To the contrary, most of the figures found on the Man of the Year roster—among them Franklin Roosevelt, Joseph Stalin, Winston Churchill, and Charles de Gaulle—were people of considerably more than transient notoriety. It is also worth adding that remembrance many years after one's moment on the public stage is not the only litmus test of greatness. One has only to read about Hugh Johnson and the evangelistic fervor with which he fired America's will to reshape her depression-ridden economy of the 1930s to know that, remembered or not, he certainly did leave a lasting mark. In short, it is undeniably true that hindsight examination of a given twelve-month period in our past will sometimes produce a Man of the Year quite different from the one selected at the time. But, in a sense, that is not as relevant, and certainly not as historically revealing, as the choice that was made within the context of the moment itself.

Figure 9. *TIME* cover of Wallis Warfield Simpson (Duchess of Windsor), January 4, 1937
Original art by Dorothy Wilding (lifedates unknown)

1. *TIME*, May 17, 1963, pp. 59–70.
2. *Ibid.*, May 10, 1963, p. 11.
3. *Ibid.*, March 3, 1967, November 3, 1967, May 24, 1968.
4. Robert T. Elson, *Time Inc.: The Intimate History of a Publishing Enterprise, 1923–1941*, vol. 1 (New York, 1968), pp. 166–67; *TIME*, December 20, 1968, p. 9.

5. *TIME*, December 3, 1934, pp. 4, 6.
6. *Ibid.*, January 18, 1937, p. 4; December 14, 1936, p. 8.
7. *Ibid.*, December 20, 1963, p. 4; December 18, 1972, p. 15.
8. *Ibid.*, January 2, 1939, p. 2.

Figure 10. *TIME* cover of Hugh S. Johnson, January 1, 1933
Original art by O. J. Jordan (lifedates unknown)

Man of the Year 1927
Charles Augustus Lindbergh (1902–1974)

Samuel Johnson Woolf (1880–1948)

Charcoal on paper, 33.6 x 28.8 cm.
(13 1/4 x 11 1/4 in.), 1927
Germantown Friends School, Philadelphia, Pennsylvania

On May 21, 1927—just 33 hours and 30 minutes after taking off from Long Island's Roosevelt airfield—Charles Augustus Lindbergh brought his plane, the *Spirit of St. Louis*, safely down at Le Bourget airport just outside of Paris. So, his attempt to become the first human to fly the Atlantic nonstop came to its triumphant close. The technology for accomplishing this feat had long been known, and it had been only a matter of time before any number of pilots could have demonstrated its feasibility. In the eyes of the world, however, that did not diminish one jot the luster that instantly attached itself to Lindbergh's name. After being mobbed by Parisians and decorated with the Legion of Honor cross, Lindbergh was next off to London, where yet more hordes of well-wishers greeted him, and George V granted him a private audience. By June 11 he was in Washington, receiving the Distinguished Flying Cross from President Calvin Coolidge as an audience of several hundred thousand looked admiringly on. Two days later New York honored Lindbergh with a ticker-tape parade up Broadway, and the city's irrepressible mayor, Jimmy Walker—not to be outdone by a mere President—told him, "New York is yours—I give it to you. You have won it."[1]

In the next several months Lindbergh's popularity subsided, but only comparatively speaking. As he crisscrossed the nation in the *Spirit of St. Louis*, he encountered worshipful crowds everywhere. To the English observer Harold Nicholson, it seemed that 1927 had not only been a landmark year in aviation; it had also witnessed the birth of a new sect, known as the "Lindbergh religion."[2]

Like all news publications of the day, *TIME* reported Lindbergh's comings and goings of 1927 fairly assiduously. But, as already noted, its editors had never considered the aviator important enough to put him on its cover. Thus the issue reporting news of Lindbergh's landing in Paris carried in that featured spot a likeness of England's George V and his consort, Queen Mary. And the cover for the issue chronicling the ceremonies honoring him in Washington pictured General Smedley Darlington Butler, who had just gone to China with orders to protect Americans from that country's civil unrest. So it went for the rest of the year. As the incredibly popular "Lucky Lindy" went from one celebration of his accomplishment to another, those charged with making *TIME*'s cover decisions appeared to be carefully avoiding what, in retrospect, seemed to be the unavoidable. It was only when the slow news of late 1927 suggested no other cover subject to them that they finally decided to feature Lindbergh as the magazine's first "Man of the Year."[4]

As this decision was being reached at *TIME*'s New York headquarters late in 1927, the recipient of this newly invented honor was in Mexico, where he was passing the holidays with the American ambassador, Dwight Morrow. Although he had just been introduced to the ambassador's daughter Anne, no one—including Lindbergh himself—knew that he was ending the most eventful year of his life with yet another newsworthy happening—namely that in Anne Morrow he had found his future wife. Instead it appeared at the moment that there was nothing new to report about Lindbergh. As a result, the story accompanying *TIME*'s first Man of the Year cover was neither particularly long nor interesting. Taking up less than two columns of space, it began with a listing of Lindbergh's physical characteristics and ended with a statement from his mother that she had "always loved" him and thought he was "the world's greatest." In between the introduction and this decidedly unstartling conclusion, the magazine had just enough room to include a photograph of Mrs. Lindbergh, some quick references to her boy's continuing popularity, and a litany of where he had flown since his return from Paris.[5]

As for Lindbergh's cover portrait, journalist-illustrator Samuel J. Woolf

Charles A. Lindbergh
May. 27, 1927

had made the original drawing for it for the *New York Times*, which had published it back in May. Woolf happened to be on his way to Paris by ship just as Lindbergh was landing at Le Bourget, and when, a day or two later, he went with a *Times* reporter to the American embassy to draw Lindbergh, he had to plow his way through a mob, hoping to catch a glimpse of the great aviator. On finally encountering the object of all this attention, Woolf began to sketch Lindbergh's face as his reporter companion interviewed him. Recalling the moment years later, Woolf observed that he was frankly "disappointed in the new world hero" and that he found "little of the dashing romance" in this young man who was now the much-pursued celebrity of two continents.[6] So saying, however, Woolf was perhaps putting his finger on the very thing that made Lindbergh into such a glorified hero in 1927. After all, how could even the most jaded resist the delightfully refreshing irony that it had been this quiet, unprepossessing youth who had just ushered in the age of modern aviation?

1. Leonard Mosley, *Lindbergh* (Garden City, N.Y., 1976), p. 122.
2. *Ibid.*, p. 125.
3. *TIME*, May 30, 1927, pp. 13–15, 16–27; June 20, 1927, pp. 16–17.
4. *Ibid.*, December 20, 1968, p. 9.
5. *Ibid.*, January 2, 1928, p. 10.
6. Samuel J. Woolf, *Here I Am* (New York, 1941), p. 163.

Couple of the Year 1937
General Chiang Kai-shek (1887–1975)
Madame Chiang Kai-shek (born 1898?)

Samuel J. Woolf (1880–1948)

Oil on canvas, 101.6 x 76.2 cm. (40 x 30 in.), 1937
National Portrait Gallery, Smithsonian Institution; gift of the estate of Muriel Woolf Hobson
NPG.86.TC77

Among the letters arriving at *TIME* in late 1937, there was an unusually long communication penned by a physician of New York City—one Ernest A. Graupner. Although he had to confess that he was neither a monarch nor a dictator, the doctor wrote, he could—thanks to the costly reform politics of Franklin Roosevelt's New Deal—lay claim to being a "divested" interest. As such, he was now the payer of "the income tax, the undivided profits tax, the social security tax, the plus tax, the surplus tax," and, last but not least, of the "nonplused tax." Thus, Dr. Graupner declared, he was on his way to mastering the art of keeping "his ear to the ground, his sore nose to the grindstone, his eye to the future and his chin up, all at the same time." In recognition of that accomplishment, he "modestly" placed his name in nomination for *TIME*'s next Man of the Year.[1]

Though doubtless amused at the possibilities such facial acrobatics suggested for a cover portrait, the editors did not buy Graupner's proposal. Instead, they bestowed their Man of the Year title for 1937 on the world's currently most celebrated political couple, Generalissimo and Madame Chiang Kai-shek.

For nearly a decade, Chiang Kai-shek had been the ascendant power behind China's struggle for autonomy and internal stability, and his wife, the former Soong Mei-ling, had been an unusually valuable helpmate in promoting those ends. Together, they had given China its first system of sound currency and network of roads. Only a few years previously, they had also launched the so-called New Life movement, the object of which was to root out a deeply entrenched system of government graft and corruption. In short, in *TIME*'s estimation, the Chiangs had provided China with its "ablest leadership" in centuries.[2]

At the moment, however, *TIME*'s couple of the year were in severe trouble. In the previous spring, Japan had set in motion its plan to claim dominion over all of China. By year's end, its well-oiled war machine had overrun roughly one-ninth of that nation's territory. In the face of this invasion, General Chiang and his wife had eventually been forced into hiding, and their precise whereabouts, "somewhere in the Yangtze Valley," were unknown. Nevertheless, *TIME* was optimistic that the Chiangs could galvanize their people into driving out the invader. If successful, the magazine conjectured, Generalissimo Chiang Kai-shek would almost certainly go down in history as "Asia's Man of the Century."[3]

To a large extent, *TIME*'s high regard for Chiang's abilities was a reflection of editor Henry Luce's unswerving admiration for him. The son of a Presbyterian missionary, Luce had grown up in China, and he had never lost his affection and concern for the country of his youth. More to the point, he was intent that China should not be allowed to fall into the hands of a Communist leadership, which, by the mid-1930s, was becoming a distinct possibility, and, in his view, Generalissimo Chiang was the only individual who could keep that from happening. As a result, Luce never lost an opportunity to use the pages of his magazine in promoting American support for Chiang, even after it was clear that this Chinese leader had more than a few shortcomings.

The artist charged with doing the Chiangs' couple-of-the-year portrait, Samuel Woolf, was best known for his charcoal likenesses of the great and newsworthy, and for many years his black-and-white portraits had regularly appeared on *TIME*'s cover. It was only in the late 1930s, when the magazine began using color images with greater frequency, that he started to do some of his *TIME* commissions in oil. One of the chief virtues of many of his drawings was a well-defined atmospheric quality, achieved largely through skillful handling of shadow and light. His finished rendering of General Chiang and his wife clearly demonstrated that Woolf's abilities in that regard were not confined to one medium.

In reminiscences about working for *TIME* in its early days, Woolf recalled that chaos routinely reigned at the fledgling magazine's New York offices. This lack of order led to a helter-skelter system of bookkeeping, which often meant that Woolf received payment for his work long after it was due.[4] Apparently that did not put the artist out to any great extent, and he continued to do covers for *TIME* through the 1930s.

1. *TIME*, December 13, 1937, p. 10.
2. *Ibid.*, January 3, 1938, p. 14.
3. *Ibid.*, pp. 14, 16.
4. Woolf, *Here I Am*, pp. 145–46.

Man of the Year 1938
Adolf Hitler (1889–1945)

Rudolph Charles von Ripper (1905–1960)

Etching, 39.7 x 29.8 cm. (15 5/8 x
11 11/16 in.), 1938
Prints Collection, The New York Public Library

By 1938 Adolf Hitler's pledges for a revitalized and all-powerful German state had made him Germany's undisputed dictator. In pursuance of those promises, he began the year by marching his army into Austria and proclaiming it part of his new Aryan empire. By late September British Prime Minister Neville Chamberlain and French Premier Edouard Daladier were seated with him at a table in Munich, granting their consent to his occupation of Czechoslovakia's Sudetenland. These two conquests, combined with Germany's massive buildup of armaments and its increasingly blatant persecution of Jews, had virtually guaranteed that Hitler would be *TIME*'s Man of the Year in 1938. One subscriber, however, predicted that the magazine would lack the courage to make this choice, and another pleaded for avoiding it altogether by leaving the cover of its first issue of 1939 blank.[1]

Implicit in both these comments was an assumption that *TIME*'s annual designation of a Man of the Year had become an honor reserved only for the virtuous. But that was not the case. In the end, the magazine's editors had no hesitation whatsoever about recognizing Germany's expansionist dictator as the individual who had most dominated the news of the past twelve months.

The question of how Hitler should be portrayed on *TIME*'s cover proved to be a more difficult matter. Initially the magazine had intended to use a color photograph, showing the German Führer in a dignified and rather flattering light. But its publisher, Ralph Ingersoll, feared that such treatment would suggest "tacit endorsement" of the appallingly aggressive *enfant terrible* who seemed to be leading Europe toward another war. So, without consulting boss Henry Luce, Ingersoll went in search of an alternative, and he found it in an etching, recently published in Paris by the Austrian-born artist Rudolph C. von Ripper.[2]

Jailed by German authorities as a result of his caricature attacks on the new Nazi order, Ripper had gone to France shortly after his release from prison in 1934.[3] There he had published *Écrasez l'infame*, a portfolio of prints decrying Hitler and his oppressions. By late 1938 the artist had arrived in the United States, and it was from this series of etchings that Ingersoll finally selected his Man of the Year portrait. Thus, when *TIME*'s subscribers received their issue of January 2, 1939, they found on its cover the reproduction of an image that Ripper had titled "The Hymn of Hate." Showing the German dictator seated at a pipe organ as victims of his regime hung from a structure reminiscent of torture wheels used in the persecution of early Christians, the illustration accomplished exactly what Ingersoll had wanted, and then some: No one—not even the least sophisticated—would ever interpret this picture as a favorable commentary on Hitler.

While Ingersoll was pleased with the cover's impact, his superior, Henry Luce, definitely was not. When he summoned Ingersoll to his office for a confrontation on the matter, it was an uncomfortable encounter indeed. Luce's quarrel, of course, was not with the cover's point of view. Rather, it lay in the fact that Ingersoll had turned *TIME*'s most important pictorial feature into an editorial page. According to Ingersoll years later, Luce's face was bone-white through much of the interview. After establishing Ingersoll's sole responsibility for the cover, Luce exclaimed, "Have you any idea what you've done? A basic tradition destroyed . . . everything I've built . . . in one gesture." A prolonged silence followed. Then Luce uttered the words "Spilt milk." With that, the meeting ended, and Luce never mentioned the cover to Ingersoll again.[4]

1. *TIME*, December 12, 1938, p. 6.
2. W. A. Swanberg, *Luce and His Empire* (New York, 1972), p. 160. A slightly varying account of the Hitler cover appears in Elson, *Time Inc.*, vol. 1, pp. 370–71.
3. "Rudolph C. von Ripper," *Art in America* 49, no. 1 (1961): 107; vertical files of American artists, Library of the National Portrait Gallery and National Museum of American Art.
4. Roy Hoopes, *Ralph Ingersoll* (New York, 1985), p. 182.

Man of the Year 1941
Franklin D. Roosevelt (1882–1945)

Ernest Hamlin Baker (1889–1975)

Watercolor on paper, 36.8 x 32.3 cm.
(14 1/2 x 12 3/4 in.), 1941
Harry Ransom Humanities Research
Center, The University of Texas at
Austin, Iconography Collection

By the first week of December 1941, *TIME*'s Man of the Year selection for its issue of January 5, 1942, had been set—or so its editors thought. Then on Sunday, December 7, as Japanese warplanes rained bombs on America's Pacific fleet at Pearl Harbor, the magazine's decision to feature auto magnate Henry Ford as the most newsworthy figure of 1941 suddenly unraveled. Within days the nation was officially at war with Japan and Germany. Beside this earthshaking event, the man who, in the past twelve months, had masterfully converted his plant facilities from car-making to war production in support of the nation's lend-lease program to war-torn Britain simply did not seem all that important. The focus was now on Washington and, more particularly, on President Roosevelt, who faced the task of guiding us through the new crisis. So it was that Henry Ford lost his chance to be *TIME*'s Man of the Year. Instead, the face found on the magazine's first cover of 1942 belonged to Franklin D. Roosevelt.[1]

This was the third time that Roosevelt had been so honored, and it marked a new era in the not-always-happy relationship between the President and America's leading newsweekly. Roosevelt had been a reader of *TIME* since its founding, and in 1923 he had penned a long and quite complimentary letter to the magazine. Among the things he liked best about this new publication, he said, was the "occasional disguised editorial" that crept into some of its objective reporting. As President, however, FDR became increasingly disenchanted with that subtle trick when he found it routinely used to criticize his administration. In November 1941, when *TIME* insinuated that Chile's President Pedro Aguirre had a stronger-than-average penchant for alcohol, Roosevelt finally had had enough. Forced to make an official diplomatic apology to Chile for *TIME*'s slur, FDR shed his normally shrewd reticence in such things and, at a press conference, lit out at the magazine for jeopardizing America's good relations with a friendly government. It was *TIME*'s turn to seethe a bit now. But, with the advent of Pearl Harbor a few weeks later and America's entry into World War II, the rancor subsided on both sides. Soon Henry Luce was writing FDR that it was his magazine's "dearest wish . . . to tell the story of absolute victory under your leadership."[2]

The Man of the Year image that ushered in this re-dawning of sweetness and light was the work of Ernest Hamlin Baker, who in the past two years had become *TIME*'s most frequently used cover maker. Baker never drew his likenesses from life and, in fact, staunchly claimed that doing so would have produced a less satisfactory product. Instead he began by studying a myriad of photographs showing his subject in as many lights and from as many angles as possible. From these he produced a preliminary drawing which he called a "facial map" and which, when completed, looked something like a minute anatomical examination of all of his subject's muscles and wrinkles. In turn, the "map" became the tracing model for his final rendering, which the artist cautiously built up with thin color washes. The result was a meticulously painted image, where almost every discernible physical aspect of his subject's face was apparent in one degree or another.

As FDR's 1941 Man of the Year portrait indicates, Baker was the most literally realistic artist who ever worked for the magazine. He was also the first illustrator to use symbolic backgrounds in his cover images. In the case of FDR's likeness, he made use of that device to include the faces of Roosevelt's new wartime allies, Britain's Winston Churchill and the Soviet Union's Joseph Stalin.[3]

1. Robert T. Elson, *The World of Time Inc.: The Intimate History of a Publishing Enterprise, 1941–1960*, vol. 2 (New York, 1973), p. 5; *TIME*, January 5, 1942, p. 59.
2. Elson, *Time Inc.*, vol. 1, pp. 480–85.
3. Guy Rowe, "Those Time Covers by Baker," *The American Artist* 7 (February 1943): 29–31, 39; Ernest Hamlin Baker, "A New Approach to Journalistic Portraits," *The American Artist* 20 (February 1956): 42–43, 68–71.

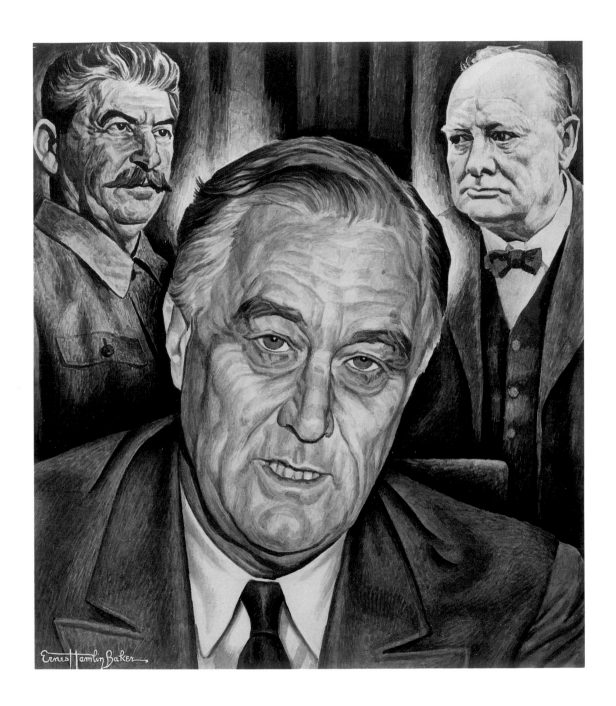

Man of the Year 1943
Joseph Stalin (1879–1953)

Boris Artzybasheff (1899–1965)

Gouache on board, 26.7 x 23.8 cm.
(10 1/2 x 9 3/8 in.), 1942
Courtesy of the Syracuse University
Art Collections

With nearly the whole world plunged into war and the daily news filled with reports of Axis and Allied troop movements in Asia, Europe, and Africa, it was inevitable that the main distinction of 1942's Man of the Year should be directly related to these conflicts. Nor is it surprising that *TIME* found itself faced that year with an unusually long list of worthies from which to make its final selection. Among others, there was German General Erwin Rommel who, despite his defeat at El Alamein, still held strong field positions in North Africa. Then, too, there was his American opponent, General Dwight D. Eisenhower, who had just established footholds at Casablanca, Oran, and Algiers. Among the candidates in Asia and the Pacific were America's Admiral William Halsey, orchestrator of the recent Allied victory at Guadalcanal, and Japan's Tomoyuki, who had driven the British from Singapore and the United States from Bataan. But, as far as *TIME* was concerned, there was one figure in this drama of offensives and counteroffensives whose accomplishments had eclipsed them all. In the past twelve months, America's Soviet ally, Joseph Stalin, had led his country through its grimmest hour. As Hitler's army rolled across Soviet borders gulping up mile after mile of territory, he had miraculously managed—on sometimes only the slenderest of resources—to maintain civilian morale and to keep his fighting forces intact. By year's end, his soldiers were delivering a resounding defeat to the Germans at Stalingrad. From this point on, as long as there were German forces in the Soviet Union, they would be largely on the defensive.

In claiming the Man of the Year title in 1942, Stalin was doing so for the second time. When he had taken that honor back in 1939, however, he had been allied to Adolf Hitler. But the friendly understanding of mutual nonaggression between the German and Soviet dictators had proven fragile at best. With Hitler's invasion of Russian territory in mid-1941, it quickly came to an end, and when America joined the war to subdue Germany at the end of that year, Stalin became her ally.

Predictably Stalin's shift from one side to another in the European conflict altered America's perception of him. Emblematic of that change was the contrast between his two Man of the Year images. When Ernest Hamlin Baker portrayed the Soviet leader for *TIME*'s cover of January 1, 1940, he had endowed his subject's smiling features with a somewhat demon-like aspect. Three years later—portrayed this time by artist Boris Artzybasheff—Stalin's face had a decidedly more heroic cast to it. As one *TIME* reader—possessed with an unusually good visual memory—suggested, it seemed as if the Soviet dictator had, in the space of thirty-six months, graduated from the ranks of the "satanic" and entered into the exalted company of the "Christlike."[1]

1. *TIME*, January 25, 1940, p. 10.

15

Man of the Year 1947
George C. Marshall (1880–1959)

Ernest Hamlin Baker (1889–1975)

Watercolor on board 27.2 x 23.5 cm.
(10 3/4 x 9 1/4 in.), 1947
George C. Marshall Research Foundation, Lexington, Virginia

When General George C. Marshall became *TIME*'s Man of the Year in 1943, he was serving as the American military's chief of staff. His competence in that position at this crucial moment in our history was unassailable, and in its issue of January 4, 1944, the magazine hailed him as "the indispensable man." It also, in so many words, characterized him as a modern-day Cincinnatus who, though masterful in war, was at heart a peace-loving civilian.[1] The description was remarkably apt. When World War II drew to a close in 1945, Marshall did not delay long his announcement that he was resigning as chief of staff. Within months he was on his way to China as President Harry Truman's personal envoy, charged with negotiating a peaceful compromise between that country's warring Communist and non-Communist factions.

Marshall was not successful in this mission, but it was the enormous difficulty of the situation rather than the man himself that accounted for the failure. In January of 1947, shortly after his return to the United States, Truman named him secretary of state. So began what may well have been the most fruitful year of Marshall's career. With the countries of war-torn Europe in desperate economic straits and many of them threatened with Soviet-inspired Communist takeovers, America's new chief diplomat moved with self-contained assurance toward alleviating this peacetime crisis. It was largely on his advice—and in his words as well—that Truman announced in the spring a costly aid program to Greece and Turkey, where the possibility of Communist coups seemed almost certain. In doing so, the President gave voice to what was quickly termed the Truman Doctrine for containing Communist aggression. But Marshall's finest moment of 1947—the one that would make him Man of the Year for a second time—was yet to come. On June 7, speaking at Harvard's commencement, the secretary of state laid out his blueprint for rebuilding Europe with massive injections of American aid. The idea had no historical precedent to prove its wisdom, and it had been set forth with no advance fanfare, in a forum far removed from any seat of political power. Nevertheless, it gave hope to a situation that until now had seemed hopeless. Within days the Marshall Plan, to reconstruct the political and economic institutions of a dangerously unstable continent, was being embraced on both sides of the Atlantic as the Free World's antidote to Communist aggression.

In its 1947 Man of the Year article, *TIME* painted Marshall as an unprepossessingly avuncular individual. In a way, that seemed to be sharply at odds with the ambitious scope of the proposal that had made him Man of the Year, and that would prove to be perhaps the most profoundly successful experiment in international cooperation ever attempted. But beneath the quiet exterior was an unswerving idealism and drive that made the pinstriped Marshall as indispensable to 1947 as the khakied Marshall had been to 1943.

1. *TIME*, January 3, 1944, pp. 16, 18.

Man of the Half-Century 1949
Winston Churchill (1874–1965)

Ernest Hamlin Baker (1889–1975)

Watercolor on board, 29.8 x 26.7 cm.
(11 3/4 x 10 1/2 in.), 1949
National Portrait Gallery, Smithsonian
Institution; gift of Time, Inc.
NPG.78.TC305

As the twentieth century approached its halfway mark in late 1949, *TIME*'s editors decided that, come the first of the new year, they would not be announcing a Man of the Year. Instead, the magazine would feature on its cover of January 2, 1950, the Man of the Half-Century. Singling someone out for this distinction was clearly a more tricky problem than simply naming the individual who had dominated the news of the past twelve months. Reflecting that difficulty, the reader nominations that year ranged everywhere from existentialist Jean-Paul Sartre and psychiatrist Sigmund Freud to the atomic scientist J. Robert Oppenheimer and humorist Will Rogers. In the end, the tally of subscriber votes favored Franklin D. Roosevelt and Winston Churchill, and the magazine settled on Churchill.[1]

Doubtless Churchill's attraction for those making the final choice at *TIME* lay partly in the fact that, unlike FDR, Churchill was still alive. Moreover, as *TIME*'s article on its Man of the Half-Century pointed out, Churchill had begun the twentieth century as a personage of some renown and notoriety, and was at its midway point an individual of yet greater stature. Most important, however, in the past fifty years, from the close of England's Boer War to the onset of the Cold War, he had been both a close observer and an active participant in more of the world's triumphs and disasters than probably any other person, alive or dead. Whatever the event—be it World War I, the Russian Revolution, or Hitler's rise and fall—the pugnaciously slouching Churchill had been in the thick of it, predicting, criticizing, acting and, with his unmatched gift for verbal eloquence, inspiring.

Despite the heavy pre-choice favoring of Churchill, many of the subscribers, reacting to his selection after it had been made, clearly did not share *TIME*'s thinking in the matter. In the post-mortem days of January 1950, one reader summarized his outrage with "You damned Tories," while another dismissed the magazine's staff as a bunch of "damn fools." "Your choice," wrote a third, "still has me in anger and disbelief . . . when my subscription expires in a few weeks I shall not renew—and with deep pleasure." Against these brickbats *TIME* could at least draw comfort from the California reader who thought so well of its Man of the Half-Century article that she had carefully stowed her copy of it with the other cherished family heirlooms that were to be left to her children.[2]

1. *TIME*, December 19, 1949, p. 3; December 26, 1949, pp. 2, 3.
2. *Ibid.*, January 23, 1950, pp. 4, 6.

Man of the Year 1957
Nikita Khrushchev (1894–1971)

Boris Artzybasheff (1899–1965)

Tempera and polymer on masonite,
40.6 x 32.8 cm. (16 x 12 7/8 in.), 1957
National Portrait Gallery, Smithsonian
Institution; gift of Time, Inc.
NPG.78.TC514

It was December 1957 and, after years of thinking that their country reigned supreme in the field of advanced space technology, Americans were feeling as if their leaders had somehow misled them in that regard. In October the Soviet Union had launched its Sputnik—the first manmade satellite to orbit the earth. Several weeks later her scientists were sending up Sputnik II, and this time there was a dog inside to test the effects of space travel on a living creature. Accomplished against the backdrop of America's recent failure to set its own Vanguard satellite aloft, these feats raised in this country a wave of pained self-examination into the factors that had left us choking on the fumes of the Soviets' jet-fueled triumphs. It had also made many subscribers to *TIME* aware that, like it or not, their favorite weekly's choice for Man of the Year would have to be Soviet leader Nikita Khrushchev. Or, as one grieved reader put it in his nomination letter, "It is Nikita—Damn it all."[1]

Khrushchev's Man of the Year designation did not hinge entirely on Sputniks I and II, however. All in all, it had been an unusually good twelve months for the Soviet premier. On the domestic front, he had begun to put Russian agriculture and industry on new and quite possibly more productive footings. In the realm of foreign relations, he could lay claim to achieving warmer ties with China and a substantially stronger network of friends in the Middle East. He could also take satisfaction in knowing that he had finally succeeded in halting the growing disaffection between the Soviet Union and its Eastern European satellites.

Clearly Khrushchev's Man of the Year cover portrait by Boris Artzybasheff was meant to be a reflection of all these successes. Thus the Russian-born artist, who had fled his homeland just as Khrushchev was joining the Bolsheviks' Red Guard back in 1917, showed his subject wearing a Kremlin-shaped crown and fondly gazing at his reflection in the shiny model of Sputnik. Like the account of Khrushchev found inside the magazine, the likeness at the same time had a slightly acerbic edge to it, and to a large extent, the gloating bravado of Khrushchev's smile echoed *TIME*'s verbal characterization of him as a self-satisfied and often arrogant braggart.[2]

1. *TIME*, December 2, 1957, p. 2.
2. *Ibid.*, January 6, 1958, p. 16.

20

21

Man of the Year 1958
Charles de Gaulle (1890–1970)

Bernard Buffet (born 1928)

Oil on canvas, 101 x 74.2 cm. (39 3/4 x 29 1/4 in.), 1958
National Portrait Gallery, Smithsonian Institution; gift of Time, Inc.
NPG.78.TC327

Almost invariably, *TIME*'s Man of the Year portraits—and for that matter its cover likenesses in general—are commissioned quite close to the date of their intended publication. But, in the case of 1958's Man of the Year, Charles de Gaulle, the magazine sensed in the spring of 1958 that, although this retired French general and politician did not figure prominently in the news at the moment, he soon would. Accordingly its editors commissioned his countryman, Bernard Buffet, to make a portrait of him against the not-too-distant day when de Gaulle might emerge as an eminently ripe choice for Man of the Year.[1]

In doing so, it was not as if there were no signs indicating that de Gaulle might soon be reentering public life. By early May, France was in the throes of a deep domestic crisis, and, with its African colonies in revolt and its finances in disarray, it was clearly due for a drastic political overhaul. More to the point, it was in desperate need of a leader around whom all Frenchmen could rally. It appeared to *TIME* that the one individual fitting that description was General Charles de Gaulle, the man who had been the much-revered embodiment of a free and independent France during the dark days of Hitler's occupation. This judgment soon proved correct. At the end of May, de Gaulle was taking control as Premier of France's chaotic Fourth Republic. By the year's end, having accepted office on the understanding that his policies would not be opposed by the normally argumentative French Parlement, he had worked miracles. Under his iron-willed guidance, the country had reformed its monetary system, instituted a deficit-reducing budget, and overhauled its judiciary. It had also redrawn its constitution and was well on its way to coming to terms with the rebelling Algerians.

During his schooling at France's military academy, Saint-Cyr, de Gaulle's elongated face and unusually great height had earned him the nickname "big asparagus." Buffet's Man of the Year portrait gives credibility to the aptness of that sobriquet. At the same time, it provides a sense of the "solemn hauteur" that the artist saw in his subject and that he, along with the majority of French people, interpreted as the outward sign of de Gaulle's magical ability to provide political stability. Writing of the portrait, after its long-delayed publication in January 1959, one *TIME* reader said: "Every time I look at it, I am reminded of those mysterious monoliths on Easter Island."[2]

1. *TIME*, January 5, 1959, p. 15.
2. *Ibid.*, pp. 15, 29; January 26, 1959, p. 4.

Man of the Year 1959
Dwight D. Eisenhower (1890–1969)

Bernard Safran (born 1924)

Oil on masonite, 61 x 44.5 cm. (24 x 17 1/2 in.), 1959
National Portrait Gallery, Smithsonian Institution; gift of Time, Inc.
NPG.78.TC349

Being named Man of the Year has never guaranteed that *TIME*'s article on the recipient of this honor would be free of criticism. But, when President Dwight D. Eisenhower received that designation for the second time in 1959, the chronicle of his recent accomplishments could only be described as an unalloyed panegyric. Eisenhower, the article declared with no perhaps or maybe, was "the world's best-known, best-liked citizen." From there, things only got better. After a laudatory cataloguing of the highlights of Ike's seventh year as President, the piece closed with the prediction that: "The forces for freedom fired by 1959's Man of the Year would change the lives of millions of grandchildren and great-grandchildren in an epochal historic way. And men of hope might have new reason to believe that tomorrow's world had a better than even chance."[1]

To some extent, the praise for Eisenhower was objectively understandable. In the past year, his landmark conference with Nikita Khrushchev at Camp David, his talks in Paris with major Western allies, and his immensely successful visits to the capitals of Africa, southern Europe, and Asia had produced the impression that he was personally leading the world away from the saber-rattling diplomacy of the Cold War into a new era of international détente. The accolades, however, were also a reflection of Henry Luce's unusually deep veneration for 1959's Man of the Year. When Eisenhower wrote *TIME*'s founder that he was almost too embarrassed by the article's praises even to say thank you, Luce affectionately answered: *The story* [was] *written from the heart as well as from the head of all concerned. Let me add personally that one of the deep satisfactions of my life is that I once went all out in advocacy of a certain man for the Presidency . . . and after seven years can say that I never for a moment regretted it.*[2]

Unfortunately, the future sometimes has an unpleasant habit of canceling out positive accomplishments in a startlingly short time. In April of 1960, the hopes raised by Eisenhower's international successes of the previous year were suddenly dashed by the downing of an American U-2 spy plane within Soviet territory. Not surprisingly, the American justification of the incident did not satisfy the Soviets. As a result, the May summit meeting—between Eisenhower, Khrushchev, Britain's Prime Minister Macmillan, and France's President de Gaulle—was aborted before it began. Soon it was back to Cold War politics as usual.

1. *TIME*, January 4, 1960, pp. 12, 16.
2. Elson, *World of Time Inc.*, vol. 2, p. 460.

Bonn

London

Paris

Washington

Bernard Safran

25

Man of the Year 1961
John F. Kennedy (1917–1963)

Pietro Annigoni (born 1910)

Watercolor on paper, 78.5 x 58.7 cm.
(30 7/8 x 23 1/8 in.), 1961
National Portrait Gallery, Smithsonian
Institution; gift of Time, Inc.
NPG.78.TC501

In December 1961 John F. Kennedy was coming to the end of his first year as President. The second-youngest individual ever to occupy the Oval Office, he had embarked on his duties with a "can-do-anything" outlook, and he had fully expected to receive endorsement for his programs with much the same rapidity that his hero, Franklin D. Roosevelt, had for his reforms back in the early days of the New Deal. As many of his predecessors discovered, however, he soon found that the immense powers and prestige of the presidency did not necessarily ensure instant results. But Kennedy was a quick learner. By year's end, although he had had to accept congressional defeats in such areas as aid to public education and medical care for the aged, he could nevertheless find solace in the fact that Congress had given him all of what he asked for in the way of a new Federal housing program and most of what he had sought for the buildup of military defense. More important, as far as *TIME* was concerned, Kennedy's capacities for leadership had matured, and he seemed better equipped now to deal with the realities of the nation's highest office. It was this growth, combined with his limited successes, that prompted the magazine to name him 1961's Man of the Year.[1]

For Kennedy's Man of the Year portrait, *TIME* decided that a special treatment was in order. By mid-December the magazine was flying the famous Italian painter Pietro Annigoni to America for sittings with Kennedy in Washington. When the artist began studying his subject in the White House, he found the President quite different from what he had expected. Here was not the broadly smiling, cocksure man of the campaign trails and state dinners, but rather a more serious and thoughtful individual—looking somewhat weighed down by the burdens of his job. After hours of scrutinizing his sitter working at his desk, Annigoni concluded that it should be this more sober dimension of the Kennedy personality that he would capture in his painting. In the finished likeness, therefore, the artist gave *TIME* readers Kennedy as he appeared in the course of his working days—slightly disheveled and earnestly deliberating with his advisers.[2]

Annigoni was not unaccustomed to controversy over his work, but perhaps he had not bargained for the great protest that followed *TIME*'s publication of his Kennedy likeness on January 5, 1962. "Any 'artist,'" railed one reader, "who can make a portrait of our president look like one of Quasimodo . . . should be boiled in his own oils." "Though I approve of your choice of President Kennedy as Man of the Year," complained another, "his portrait . . . makes me recoil . . . like Macbeth upon seeing the ghost of Banquo." One of the shortest commentaries came from a subscriber in Key West, Florida, who dismissed Annigoni's handiwork as "A jaundiced Dracula, in ragpicker's clothing on a background of bile!" In the face of these assaults, Annigoni remained unflappable. When asked by *TIME* to comment in his own defense, he remarked that, "from the point of view of interpretation, I quite agree with myself."[3]

Although many *TIME* readers found the portrait of Kennedy thoroughly repugnant, the newsstand sale of the magazine's January 5 issue proved unusually brisk. Evaluating that fact against the marketing experts' claim that a periodical's salability rose and fell with the attractiveness of its covers, it would seem that something was amiss: Either this longstanding Madison Avenue axiom was untrue, or Annigoni's likeness had not put off nearly so many readers as *TIME*'s angry letters to the editor suggested.[4]

1. *TIME*, January 5, 1962, p. 9.
2. *Ibid.*, p. 5.

3. *Ibid.*, January 12, 1962, p. 2; January 19, 1962, pp. 6, 11.
4. *Ibid.*, January 19, 1962, p. 11.

Man of the Year 1962
Pope John XXIII (1881–1963)

Bernard Safran (born 1924)

Oil on masonite, 58.4 x 41.2 cm. (23 x 16 1/4 in.), 1962
National Portrait Gallery, Smithsonian Institution; gift of Time, Inc.
NPG.78.TC676

Pope John XXIII had assumed leadership of the Catholic Church in 1958, and it was commonly thought at the time that, given his advanced age, his term in office would not prove particularly noteworthy. As *TIME*'s 1962 Man of the Year article pointed out, it was anything but that. Although his Vatican Council II was not yet over, it was already obvious that this meeting of some 2,500 clerical leaders from around the world was remaking the Church in a new and more liberal image. By the adjournment of its first session in December, it was, for example, apparent that the Catholic Church was about to trade its rigid, centuries-old hierarchy for a more democratic structure, in which both laity and lower-ranking clerics would have significantly greater voice. It was also clear that out of the council was coming a new ecumenism intended to break down the once-insurmountable barriers between Catholicism and other Christian faiths. The credit for these and other far-reaching reforms of an institution claiming a membership of 900 million souls could be shared by many. But Pope John XXIII had been their main inspiration, and without his determination to guide the Church toward drastic change, there would have been no Vatican II at all. In short, although 1962 had seen momentous events in world politics and space technology, it was *TIME*'s considered opinion that history books of the future would look back on this year and judge John XXIII as the one individual who had done most to alter humanity's spiritual life and, in turn, the complexion of the world in general.

To paint the Pope's Man of the Year portrait, *TIME* enlisted one of its most frequent cover makers of the late 1950s and early 1960s, Bernard Safran. It is not known whether the earthbound simplicity of the finished image was a consciously sought effect that had been mutually agreed upon beforehand by artist and editors. Nevertheless, this quality seemed to be emblematic of the quiet unpretentiousness that the Roman Pontiff had brought to his office and that had made him markedly indifferent to—and at times even embarrassed by—the exalting titles and prerogatives that came with his position.

Man of the Year 1963
Martin Luther King, Jr. (1929–1968)

Robert Vickrey (born 1926)

Tempera on paper, 37.5 x 28.5 cm.
(14 3/4 x 11 1/4 in.), 1963
National Portrait Gallery, Smithsonian
Institution; gift of Time, Inc.
NPG.78.TC517

On New Year's Day, 1863, Abraham Lincoln had signed his executive decree, known forever after as the Emancipation Proclamation. Although technically applicable only to the Confederate states, the document had, for all intents and purposes, declared an end to the enslavement of blacks everywhere in America. But the blacks' liberation from white masters was not the same as the achievement of full civil rights under the Constitution. A century after Lincoln's proclamation, *TIME* was honoring as its Man of the Year Martin Luther King, Jr., whose recent activities seemed at last to be winning for his people the long denied privileges of equal opportunity in politics, jobs, housing, and education.

In arriving at an estimation of its Man of the Year for 1963, *TIME* was hard pressed to define what made King such a compelling and successful leader of America's mid-twentieth-century civil rights movement. One of his main strengths was his speaking ability, but his choice of words and metaphors, the magazine noted, was often unfortunate. "Yet when he mounts the platform," it continued, "the actual words seem unimportant. And King, by some quality of that limpid voice or by some secret of cadence, exercises control as can few others over his audience, black or white."[1]

But, if the sources of his galvanizing appeal were difficult to pinpoint, the magnitude of his accomplishments was not. In the year just past, King had spearheaded protests in that most racially segregated of cities, Birmingham, Alabama, where the violence of the white opposition had only served to heighten sympathy for his civil rights cause. Inspired by King, demonstrations against racial discrimination spread to hundreds of other cities north and south. In the late summer King and a host of other civil rights leaders were at the Lincoln Memorial in Washington addressing a throng of 200,000-plus, who had come to the capital seeking Federal support for the redress of black grievances. By year's end, it was beginning to seem all but certain that America's racial relationships were about to change drastically, and that the United States Congress would soon be providing the legal framework for a black-white equality that until now had seemed but a remote dream.

The artist hired to do King's portrait for *TIME*'s issue of January 3, 1964, was Robert Vickrey, who had been doing covers for the magazine since 1957. A widely acknowledged master in the tempera medium, he was capable of producing a good likeness from photographs. Nevertheless, he much preferred to work from life sittings, and because of his admiration for King's work, Vickrey was in this instance especially anxious for a firsthand encounter. According to the artist, however, King had not always liked the way *TIME* reported his activities. As a result, he was somewhat hostile to the magazine and refused its initial request that he meet with Vickrey. But with some further cajoling, the no became yes. Shortly thereafter, Vickrey, in the company of a *TIME* reporter, was encountering King in an Atlanta, Georgia, hotel room. As the journalist plied the civil rights leader with questions, the artist anguished over getting the "almost oriental look" of his subject's eyelids right.

At one point, speaking of the many harassments he had endured in recent years, King remarked: "The IRS audits me every year. . . . I think the FBI has me tapped. I get death threats all the time. But I know my cause is good." With those last words, Vickrey has noted, "a fine look came into his eyes, and I determined to capture it."[2]

1. *TIME*, January 3, 1964, p. 14.
2. Unpublished recollections of Robert Vickrey.

Man of the Year 1964
Lyndon B. Johnson (1908–1973)

Peter Hurd (1904–1984) and Henriette Wyeth (born 1907)

Tempera on paper, 55.2 x 37.5 cm. (21 3/4 x 14 3/4 in.), 1964
National Portrait Gallery, Smithsonian Institution; gift of Time, Inc.
NPG.78.TC477

When Lyndon Johnson became *TIME*'s 1964 Man of the Year, he was just completing the most successful twelve months of his public career. Having inherited the presidency on the death of John Kennedy in late 1963, he had in the recent November election claimed this office in his own right in one of the greatest landslide victories ever recorded in the annals of presidential elections. More important, in the year preceding, his subtle skills in the handling of Congress had yielded the most sweeping civil rights legislation since the Civil War, reduced the government deficit by half, and set in motion a new Federally funded war on the nation's poverty. As 1964 drew to a close, it also looked as though Johnson's amazing talent for bending a sometimes-reluctant Congress to his will would soon produce this country's first national program of medical care for the aged.

By now, Johnson had appeared on the cover of *TIME* on nine occasions, and in the case of his Man of the Year portrait the magazine decided that his new likeness should have a distinction that would separate it from the Johnson images of covers past. To that end, *TIME*'s editors dispatched not one but two artists to record the President's features in Washington, Peter Hurd and his wife, Henriette Wyeth. In addition to the couple's eminence as two of the Southwest's most respected painters, *TIME* was doubtless aware that their choice of portraitists was a good one for yet another reason. Having met Johnson on several occasions, Hurd and Wyeth liked their subject and admired his politics. By the same token, the President had long been a fan of Hurd's New Mexico landscapes, which reminded him of the broad, arid horizons of his own native Texas. As a result, the sittings with Johnson in his office proved unusually congenial. After several hours of posing, the President personally took the two artists on a tour of the White House, in the course of which he proudly pointed to the landscape by Hurd that hung over his bedroom mantel.[1]

Even before he and his wife arrived in Washington in late 1964, Hurd knew that he wanted to capture the decidedly "Southwest" cast of Johnson's features, which he found especially apparent in his subject's firmly set jaw and narrowly squinting eyes. To highlight those traits in the finished likeness, Hurd and Wyeth placed Johnson against a sun-drenched Texas background, showing in the distance a rendering of the President's white clapboard birthplace. Initially Johnson expressed dismay with the completed portrait, noting that he particularly disliked the treatment of his eyes. Once the artists' intentions were explained, however, he warmed to it. When Hurd was invited back to the White House several months later to meet South Korean President Chung Hee Park, Johnson, with no advance warning, introduced the artist to his foreign visitor as the man designated to do his official White House portrait.[2]

Once recovered from the offhanded nature of this announcement, Hurd readily accepted the new commission. The second likeness, however, did not produce the same happy experience that the first one had. Hampered by the facts that Johnson had time for only two short sittings, and that during one he kept falling asleep, Hurd finally had to resort to presidential photographs for his model. Finally, after laboring for many hours in his New Mexico studio, the artist arrived at what he thought was a satisfactory state portrait. But, although Hurd was reasonably pleased with his efforts, the subject was unequivocally not. At a private showing of the work at Johnson's Texas ranch in 1966, the President informed Hurd that the portrait was "the ugliest thing" he had ever seen. So ended the once convivial relationship between 1964's Man of the Year and his favorite Southwest painter. When news of the incident became public, the witticism began circulating in Washington that "artists should be seen around the White House—but not Hurd."[3]

1. *TIME*, January 1, 1965, p. 13; January 13, 1967, p. 13.
2. *Ibid.*, January 13, 1967, p. 13.
3. *Ibid.*

People of the Year 1966
Twenty-Five and Under

Robert Vickrey (born 1926)

Tempera and ink on board, 55.2 x 40.6
cm. (21 3/4 x 16 in.), 1966
National Portrait Gallery, Smithsonian
Institution; gift of Time, Inc.
NPG.78.TC168

Occasionally, *TIME*'s end-of-the-year ponderings on the question of who most
shaped the events of the past twelve months has led the magazine to a Man of the
Year possessing no particular name or physical description. The first instance of
this was in 1950, when, with more than 100,000 American soldiers fighting in the
Korean conflict, the magazine's editors bestowed their Man of the Year honors on
the generic "G.I. Joe." In 1966 the Man of the Year once again had no proper
name. Instead it was a whole generation—commonly known as the "baby boomers" and described by *TIME* as "the man—and woman—of 25 and under."[1]

Assertive, idealistic, affluent, and distrustful of anyone over thirty, this
group of Americans, the magazine reported, was about to become a majority in
the country's population. Moreover, in their liberal views on sex, their concern for
social justice, and their rejection of traditional values, they seemed to be taking
society in decidedly new directions. Although *TIME* recognized that such collec-
tivizing generalities did not apply with equal force to each and every member of
the under-twenty-five generation, it could not help but think that, whatever the
changes wrought by this group, they would be both notable and positive. "With
his skeptical yet humanistic outlook, his disdain for fanaticism and his scorn for
the spurious," the magazine's analysis concluded, *the Man of the Year suggests that he
will infuse the future with a new sense of morality, a transcendent and contemporary ethic
that could infinitely enrich society. If he succeeds . . . the Man of the Year will be a man
indeed—and have a great deal of fun in the process.*[2]

Once the Man of the Year choice for 1966 had been made, *TIME*'s staff
quickly concluded that the cover image, accompanying their verbal analysis of the
baby boomers, should not be of only one individual. Nor was it appropriate, they
thought, that any of the people portrayed should be recognizable. When artist
Robert Vickrey showed his rendering of *Twenty-five and Under* to the magazine's
editors, however, one of them noted that the handsome youth dominating the
picture looked suspiciously like his creator as he might have appeared fifteen years
earlier. "Something like that might have slipped in," admitted the forty-year-old
Vickrey.[3]

Most often, the reader responses to *TIME*'s annual Man of the Year
selections have reflected gut reactions of the moment. But occasionally the choice
has inspired an observation of an unusually keen nature. "It's sad," wrote a forty-
year-old Alabama woman of the 1966 Man of the Year, "but I betcha that 25 years
from now you won't be able to tell them from us." In some respects, that
prediction may not come true. On the other hand, as a *TIME* article on the
progress of the baby boomers pointed out only recently, the maturing of this
generation over twenty years has indeed instilled it with a greater conservatism
and substantially tempered some of its once ardent impulses for social change.[4]

1. *TIME*, January 6, 1967, p. 18.
2. *Ibid.*, p. 23.
3. *Ibid.*, p. 11.
4. *Ibid.*, January 13, 1967, p. 6; May 19,
1986, pp. 22–26, 35–43.

Man of the Year 1967
Lyndon B. Johnson (1908–1973)

David Levine (born 1926)

Pen and ink on board, 26.7 x 18.8 cm.
(10 1/2 x 7 3/8 in.), 1967
National Portrait Gallery, Smithsonian
Institution; gift of Time, Inc.
NPG.78.TC475

There have been instances when *TIME*'s Man of the Year choice has reminded its readers of how quickly and radically a public figure's fortune can change. Named as 1964's Man of the Year because of his remarkable triumphs that year, President Lyndon Johnson received this honor again in 1967. But this time it was given in recognition of his failed leadership. Routinely jeered at public gatherings for escalating the Vietnam war, chastised by blacks for moving too slowly on civil rights, and hounded in Congress for his costly domestic social programs, Johnson had become one of the most bitterly maligned Presidents in the nation's history. By the fall of 1967, his popularity rating in the public polls had plummeted from a onetime peak of 80 percent to a woeful 38 percent.

In analyzing Johnson's grim situation, *TIME* hypothesized that its 1967 Man of the Year was fundamentally a capable individual who, similar to King Lear, had run afoul of his friends and his own generous intentions. But, unlike Shakespeare's Lear, the magazine speculated that Johnson might eventually reverse his current streak of ill fortune. The greatest Presidents, it reminded readers, were those who presided over periods of severe crises, and "Johnson still has a chance to stand among them."[1]

Like the article about him, Johnson's 1967 Man of the Year portrait by caricaturist David Levine found its inspiration in the tale of Lear's betrayal by his offspring. In it, the President—cast as a medieval monarch—loomed dolefully as his fellow Democrats and onetime allies—Senator Robert Kennedy and Representative Wilbur Mills—connived to erode his power. As with Lear, there was one member of Johnson's "family," however, who had remained steadfastly loyal, and tearfully clinging to his knee was his Vice-President, Hubert Humphrey.

When Levine did this drawing for *TIME*, critics were beginning to see him as heir to the nineteenth century's golden age of political caricature, when such satirists as Sir John Tenniel and Thomas Nast were wielding their rapier-like pens. His boldly drafted drawings, they said, exhibited a "murderous" and "unmerciful" wit. But, as Levine himself admitted, his powers as a pictorial commentator had definite limitations. "No government," he once remarked to an interviewer, "has ever fallen because of my caricatures."[2]

1. *TIME*, January 5, 1968, p. 22.
2. *Current Biography Yearbook, 1973*, ed.
Charles Moritz (New York, 1973), p. 21.

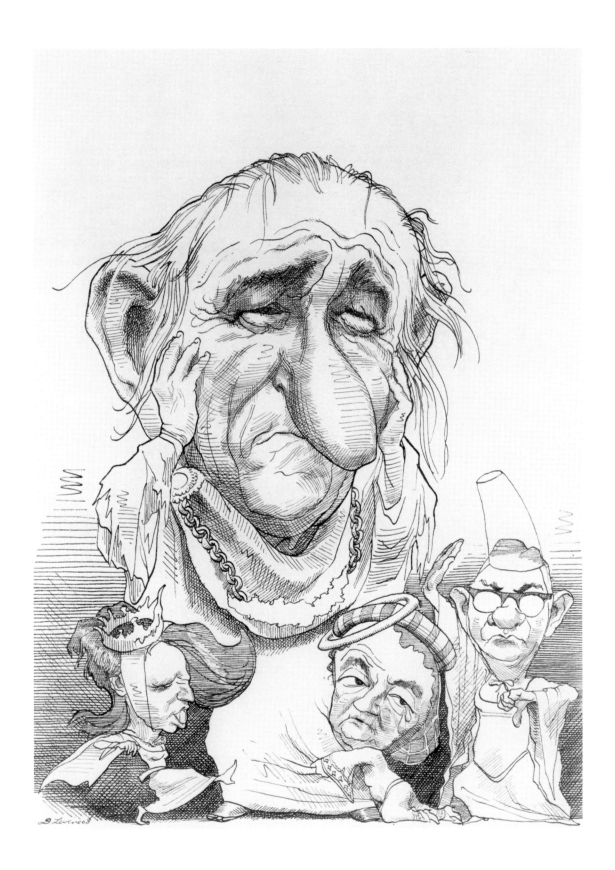

37

Men of the Year 1968

William Anders (born 1933)
Frank Borman (born 1928)
James Lovell (born 1928)

The year 1968 had witnessed the assassination of civil rights leader Martin Luther King, Jr., and, less than two months later, of presidential candidate Robert F. Kennedy. It had also seen rioting in the nation's black urban ghettos, mounting protests over the war in Vietnam, and waves of student revolts on college campuses. On the international front there had been a Soviet invasion of Czechoslovakia, an American-Soviet confrontation in the Middle East, and a rebellion of workers and youths in France that had nearly toppled the country's President, Charles de Gaulle. But, as *TIME* pointed out in its end-of-the-year summary, 1968 had ended with an event that was akin to Columbus's reaching America in 1492 and that, in the long term, was bound to overshadow these other dramatic happenings: In late December, three astronauts—William Anders, Frank Borman, and James Lovell—had embarked on the first human exploration of the moon. By Christmas Eve, while most of their fellow Americans were preparing to exchange presents around tinsel-decked evergreens, this trio of space pioneers was circling that celestial body in their Apollo 8 vehicle, which only a few years earlier had seemed to be but a remote possibility. The full implication of this achievement was not generally understood yet. But then, too, much the same had been true of Columbus's discovery when it had first become known nearly five centuries earlier. With that in mind, *TIME* could not help but conclude that out of all the people who had made news in the past twelve months, Anders, Borman, and Lovell were the hands-down choice for 1968's Man of the Year.

Given the enormity of current problems here on earth, there were many who deplored the great expense and human energy that had gone toward sending these men to the moon. At least one commentator at *TIME* was sympathetic to that point of view. Nevertheless, he was able to find value in the astronauts' feat even for those most skeptical of its worth. "The triumph of Apollo 8," he noted, *cannot erase the irony that it is easier to go to the moon than to wipe out a ghetto, easier for him to travel through space than to clean up his own polluted atmosphere, easier for him to establish cooperation in a vast technological enterprise than to establish brotherhood on a city block. Yet as man has conquered the seas, the air and other natural obstacles, he has also at each stage, in a small way, conquered part of himself. Therein lies the hope and the ultimate promise of his latest conquest.*[1]

1. *TIME*, January 3, 1969, p. 17.

Hector Garrido (born 1927)

Acrylic and tempera on masonite, 53.9 x 40 cm. (21 1/4 x 15 3/4 in.), 1968
National Portrait Gallery, Smithsonian Institution; gift of Time, Inc.
NPG.78.TC203

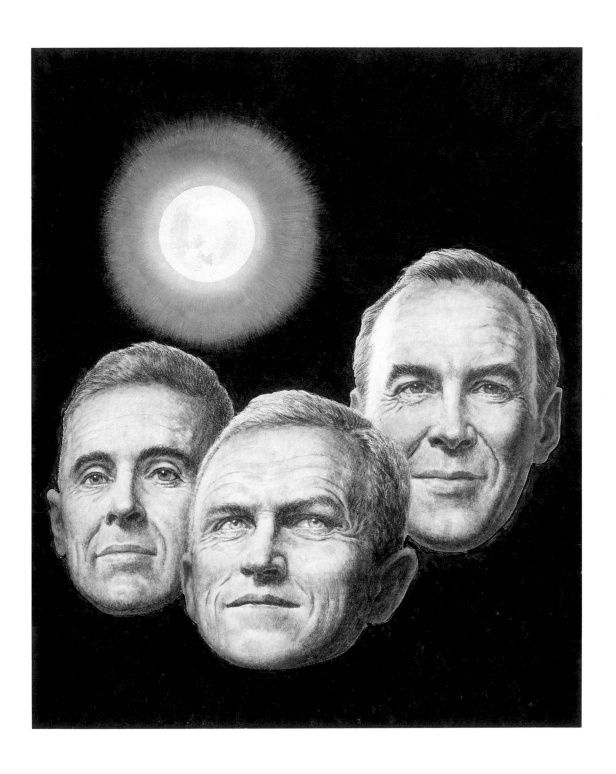

People of the Year 1969
The Middle Americans

Vin Giuliani (1930–1976)

Metal, wood, and paper collage, 51.8 x
36.5 x 12.7 cm. (20 3/8 x 14 3/8 x 5
in.), 1969
National Portrait Gallery, Smithsonian
Institution; gift of Time, Inc.
NPG.78.TC836

Some called them the "silent majority"; others referred to them as the "Middle Americans." Regardless of name, one thing about this substantial portion of the nation's citizenry was abundantly clear. Through much of the late 1960s, as violent civil-rights protests and demonstrations over the Vietnam war swept through one community after another, as cities witnessed upsurges in crime, and as the nation's youth rejected the values of their parents, this group's adherence to the traditional verities of American life seemed to be steadily losing ground.

The Middle Americans defied any attempt to categorize them as predominantly Republican or Democrat. Nevertheless, they had much in common with each other. Among other things, they were patriotic, and they had little tolerance for civil rights and antiwar dissidents such as Abbie Hoffman and Eldridge Cleaver, who asserted that the nation's political system was corrupt beyond redemption. At the same time, they generally regarded hard work and the family unit as positive goods. As a result, they had also lost patience with the hippie counterculture, which espoused communal lifestyles and cast disdainful eyes on the more traditional concepts of vocational ambition and suburban domestic tranquillity.

But, if the Middle Americans seemed to have gone into eclipse during much of the 1960s, they were by no means dead. By 1969 their voices were finally beginning to be heard above the uproar of radical dissent. Within Washington's present Nixon administration and local governments as well, their fundamentally conservative outlook was manifesting itself in more gradualistic policies in the area of black civil rights and in announced crackdowns on urban criminals. They were also making themselves felt through demonstrations of patriotism. If there was an emblem for the Middle Americans, it was the decal reproductions of the nation's flag, which they proudly affixed to their car bumpers and windowpanes.

As of late 1969, the Middle Americans' resurging influence had not led to any great or drastic change in the complexion of the nation's life. Yet politicians and sociologists were definitely starting to rediscover them as a potent factor in our unsettled society. It was in recognition of this fact that *TIME* decided to cast the Middle American as its 1969 Man of the Year.

Interestingly enough, for the cover accompanying its story of this tradition-minded segment of the population, *TIME* settled on a somewhat unconventional image. Although Vin Giuliani's stylized, mixed-media rendering of Mr. and Mrs. Middle American did not stand on the outer edge of the avant-garde, it did not share much in common with the more sedate realism that was so often associated with *TIME* covers.

One of the magazine's readers characterized Giuliani's conception of his subject as a "visual put-down" to all Middle Americans, including himself. Several other subscribers, on the other hand, took exception not so much to the cover as they did to the whole notion of making Middle Americans Man of the Year, and a man in Buffalo likened the choice to giving the scorekeeper the Most Valuable Player award. Nevertheless, there were those who were quite pleased indeed with both *TIME*'s judgment and Giuliani's artwork. As one woman put it, "My husband and I were very proud to be on the cover of your magazine. . . . You've captured in print our hopes, our ideals, our feelings, our fears and our concern."[1]

1. *TIME*, January 26, 1969, p. 2.

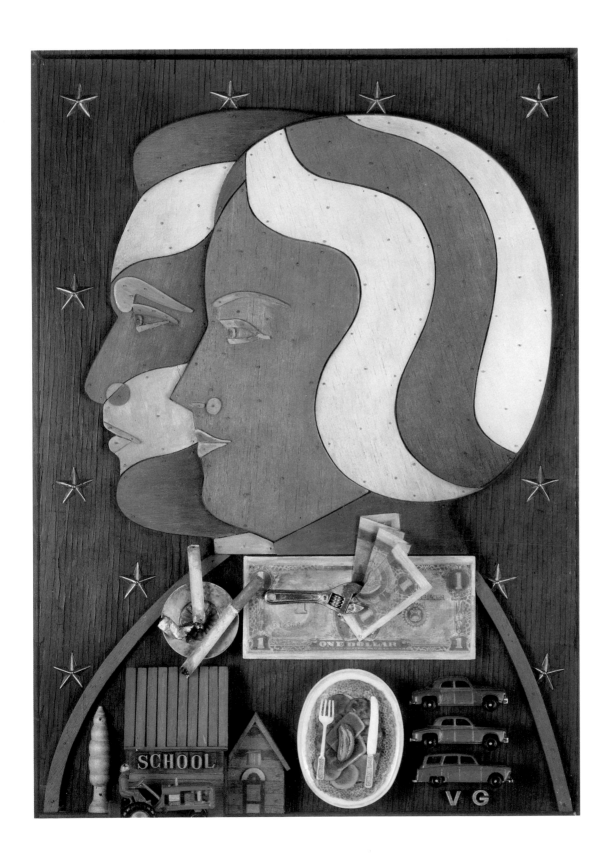

Man of the Year 1970
Willy Brandt (born 1913)

West German Chancellor Willy Brandt, *TIME* observed of its 1970 Man of the Year, had in the past twelve months signaled a new era in European diplomacy. Through talks and negotiations with the Soviet Union and its iron-curtain satellites, he stood on the verge of putting his country on a friendlier footing with Communist Europe. And in the process he seemed to be leading Europe as a whole out of the tense Cold War atmosphere of the last twenty-five years. As Brandt saw it, Germany had at times in the distant past been a bridge for understanding between Eastern and Western Europe. But since World War II it had been too preoccupied with the traumas of defeat to serve in that capacity. Now, however, Brandt was determined that West Germany should once again become a bridge and that, in doing so, it should pave the way for the détente between Communist and non-Communist Europe that for so long had been elusive. Brandt's effort in this direction, *TIME* observed, "may, of course, prove not only unworkable but also dangerous. So far, however, as the theme for a young decade, it offers immense promise for the peaceful future of Europe."[1]

George Giusti, the artist commissioned to make Brandt's Man of the Year portrait, was accustomed to working in a variety of media. But, whatever his materials, he invariably brought to them a genius for reducing his subjects to their most basic elements without diminishing the dynamic sense of their reality.[2] In no instance was this more true than in his steel and aluminum likeness of the West German Chancellor where, despite the coldness of his medium, the flesh-and-blood Brandt nevertheless seems to come through. In conceiving this piece, Giusti wanted a good portrait, but he also intended it to be a visual echo of *TIME*'s analysis of Brandt's recent accomplishments. Thus the two slightly separated pieces of metal, making up the background, were meant to represent Eastern and Western Europe. By spanning both, Brandt's features become an emblem of the role that he hoped his country would play in closing the chasm between these two geographical divisions.

George Giusti (born 1908)

Aluminum, steel, and colored paper, 34.3 x 25.2 cm. (13 1/2 x 9 7/8 in.), 1970
National Portrait Gallery, Smithsonian Institution; gift of Time, Inc.

1. *TIME*, January 4, 1971, p. 20.
2. Georgine Oeri, "George Giusti," *Graphis* 26 (1949): 148.

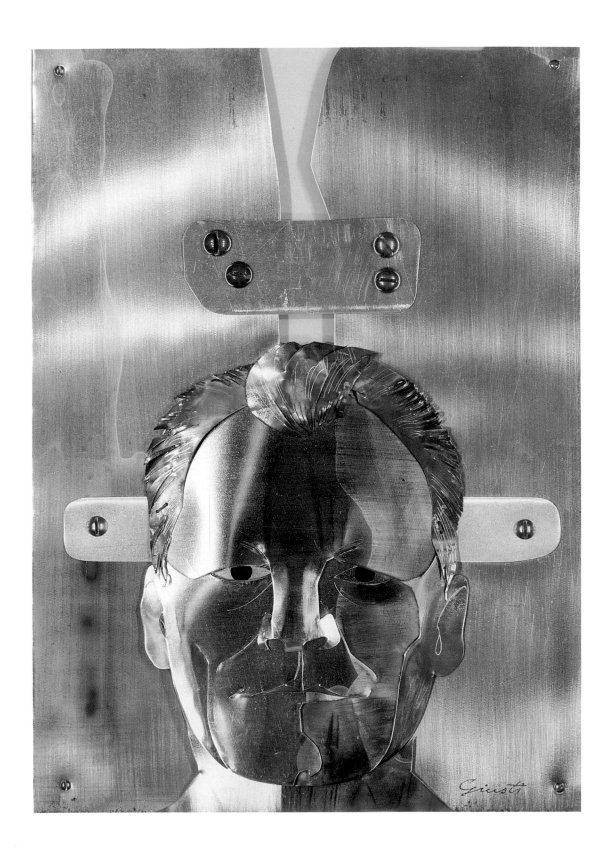

Men of the Year 1972
Richard Nixon (born 1913)
Henry Kissinger (born 1923)

Marisol (Escobar) (born 1930)

Marble, 35.5 x 53.3 x 17.7 cm. (14 x 21
x 7 in.), 1972
National Portrait Gallery, Smithsonian
Institution; gift of Time, Inc.
NPG.78.TC629

A number of American Presidents have won *TIME*'s Man of the Year title more
than once. But, as the magazine pointed out in its maiden issue of 1973, no White
House incumbent had ever claimed it for two years running. At least that was the
case until 1972, when Richard Nixon—in tandem with his National Security
Council chief, Henry Kissinger—found himself, for the second January in a row,
pictured on *TIME*'s cover as Man of the Year. In bestowing this honor on the
individual who had won it only the year before, the newsweekly's editors may
have had the uncomfortable feeling that they were becoming Johnny-one-notes.
Still, there was no escaping the fact that Nixon had, with the help of Kissinger,
signaled many new departures in American diplomacy and, in the process, once
again dominated the events of the past twelve months. In a flurry of decisive
moves, these two men had not only succeeded in opening diplomatic relations with
Communist China; they had also pressed on with the Soviets toward a new treaty
on arms limitations and managed to negotiate no less than fifteen bilateral agree-
ments promising greater international cooperation in trade, technology, and space.
In short, although the settlement of the Vietnam war that Nixon had promised
during his election campaign of 1968 still proved troublesomely elusive, the
President and his trusted Kissinger seemed to have moved a long way toward
replacing America's confrontational Cold War policies with a less anxiety-ridden
brand of international détente.

For many years the main trademark of *TIME*'s cover portraits was their
nearly photographic realism. By the early 1970s, however, the magazine had
become considerably more adventuresome in its choice of artist for that feature
spot, and its Man of the Year likeness for 1972 was a reflection of that trend. To
fashion the double image of Nixon and Kissinger, the magazine settled on the
sculptor Marisol Escobar, whose expressionistic renderings of such figures as
Charles de Gaulle and Lyndon Johnson had made her a sensation in New York's
world of contemporary art. Known professionally as simply Marisol, this taciturn
artist generally infused her work with touches of irreverent humor, and it is
difficult to escape the feeling that in carving Nixon and Kissinger she intended to
create a parody of Gutzon Borglum's Mount Rushmore renderings of Washington,
Jefferson, Lincoln, and Theodore Roosevelt.

Man of the Year 1973
John J. Sirica (born 1904)

Stanislaw Zagorski (born 1933)

Acrylic, metallic paint, and cloth on board, 48.2 x 38.1 cm. (19 x 15 in.), 1973
National Portrait Gallery, Smithsonian Institution; gift of Time, Inc.
NPG.78.TC753

Richard Nixon must have taken satisfaction in the fact that *TIME* had anointed him Man of the Year for two years running. By the end of 1973, however, the warm feeling of pride over that distinction had doubtless disappeared in the wake of revelations regarding that most convoluted series of crimes and alleged White House malfeasance known as the Watergate scandal. It was not yet known just how Nixon himself figured in the conspiracy to wiretap the Democrats' election headquarters during the presidential campaign of the previous year, or what knowledge he had of the illegal contributions that had helped to finance his overwhelming triumph at the polls. Nor was it clear what part he and some of his close advisers had played in obstructing the judicial and congressional inquiries into these crimes. But, thanks largely to the dogged persistence of a little-known Federal judge named John Sirica, who happened to preside over the trial of those charged with wiretapping Democratic headquarters, the evidence and allegations of wrongdoing among Nixon and his official White House family were growing daily. By year's end, no less than twelve presidential aides or their hirelings stood convicted for their part in the Watergate scandal; six more—including former Attorney General John Mitchell—had been indicted; and seven other figures seemed threatened with indictment on charges ranging everywhere from perjury and obstruction of justice to fraud and the solicitation of illegal campaign funds.

In uncovering the truth of this complex affair, many were instrumental. There was, for example, North Carolina Senator Sam Irvin, chairman of the congressional committee established to investigate Watergate. At the Department of Justice there was special prosecutor Archibald Cox, who had pressed hard for tapes of presidential conversations relating to the scandals and was fired for doing so. Also at Justice was Attorney General Eliot Richardson, who had supported Cox's request and resigned in protest over his subordinate's dismissal in what quickly became known as the "Saturday Night Massacre." But the man who seemed to have been most pivotal in disclosing the Watergate story was the unassuming but determined Sirica, who had used his sentencing power over those convicted of involvement in the wiretap conspiracy to extract crucial information implicating the White House in this crime. Several months later, Sirica was helping to reveal yet other dimensions of the scandal by insisting that Nixon hand over Watergate-related tapes of Oval Office conversations. Simply put, Sirica seemed to be the *sine qua non* in the unraveling of this complex drama of conspiracy, trickery, and the suborning of justice. When *TIME* settled down to selecting its Man of the Year for 1973, it should, therefore, have been a surprise to no one when he emerged as the final choice.

Even so, some of *TIME*'s readers were not happy with it. "Judge John Sirica is a despicable, contemptible, malicious man," railed one, and another informed the magazine's editors that their new Man of the Year was "as poor a selection as you have ever made." But the last word in the matter came from a subscriber in Ohio, who asked the question, knowing full well its answer: "Does anyone else . . . find it somewhat ironic that Judge John Sirica is this year's Man of the Year for having the courage to investigate what last year's Man of the Year and his . . . advisers did."[1]

1. *TIME*, January 26, 1974, p. 6; February 4, 1974, p. 11.

Man of the Year 1976
James Earl (Jimmy) Carter (born 1924)

James Wyeth (born 1946)

Watercolor on paper, 35.5 x 28 cm. (14 x 11 1/16 in.), 1976
National Portrait Gallery, Smithsonian Institution; gift of Time, Inc.
NPG.78.TC288

In the early days of presidential-election year 1976, one of the most frequently heard quips on the campaign trail was "Jimmy Who?" In less than twelve months, that knowingly sardonic query—capsulizing the supposed fruitlessness of Jimmy Carter's attempt to capture the nation's highest office—had been answered in a way few had expected. Defying all the time-honored axioms of American political wisdom, Carter had toppled better-known presidential hopefuls from within his own Democratic party in the primaries, developed a unique brand of conservative populism to which voters seemed susceptible, and become his party's standard-bearer. Most important, this once obscure Georgia governor had won the presidency itself and, in doing so, had demolished the many seasoned pundits who in January had dismissed his Oval Office aspirations as preposterous. For achieving this "political miracle" Carter received a bonus that even he had not counted on. On January 3, 1977, *TIME* declared him Man of the Year.

In its analysis of Carter, *TIME* described him as a Democrat "who often talks and thinks like a Republican," as a warm man who could nevertheless be cold, and as an individual of uncommon frankness who yet engaged sometimes in equivocation. Such contradictions made the prognosis for his performance after inaugural day a chancy proposition at best. The most one *TIME* expert would say on that point was that Carter "will be either one of the greatest presidents of the modern era or . . . a complete failure."[1]

In its Man of the Year article, *TIME* also noted that President-elect Carter had a strong preference for informality and that he intended to forego the customary morning attire and limousine at his inauguration in favor of a business suit and an unpretentious Ford. The open-collared casualness of Carter's Man of the Year portrait by Jamie Wyeth anticipated those departures from the more formal inaugural traditions. At the same time, there is a toughness about the image that seems to offer a visual equivalent to the observation of one Carter intimate that Carter's insides were made of "twisted steel cable."[2]

A third-generation member of modern-day America's best-known painting family, Wyeth arrived at his final cover image from sittings at the President-elect's home in Plains, Georgia. After he submitted the picture for publication, it was discovered that he had forgotten to sign it, and at the eleventh hour *TIME* flew him to Chicago, where the picture was being printed, to add that last finishing touch.[3]

1. *TIME*, January 3, 1977, p. 22.
2. *Ibid.*, p. 14.
3. *Ibid.*, May 15, 1978, p. 3.

49

Man of the Year 1979
Ayatollah Ruhollah Khomeini (born 1900)

Brad Holland (born 1944)

Oil on canvas, 27.9 x 20.3 cm. (11 x 8 in.), 1979
National Portrait Gallery, Smithsonian Institution; gift of Time, Inc.
NPG.84.TC122

In February 1979, the rabidly anti-American Ayatollah Ruhollah Khomeini won control of Iran. By year's end, a group of his followers had invaded the United States embassy there and seized some fifty American hostages, most of whom would remain their captives for more than a year. The rise of this seventy-nine-year-old Moslem fundamentalist and his followers' outrageous breach of traditional diplomatic protections put America to one of the severest tests of will and strategy that it had ever faced in foreign affairs. In short, as *TIME* told its readers on January 7, 1980, the Ayatollah Khomeini had amply met the magazine's Man of the Year criteria: In the past twelve months, he had without doubt been the individual who had "done the most to change the news, for better or for worse."

TIME suspected that this choice was going to offend many of its readers, and in the same issue announcing the Ayatollah as Man of the Year, the magazine's "Letter from the Publisher" sought to head off the anticipated indignation by pointing out that other decidedly unlikable figures—notably Hitler and Stalin—had also been Man of the Year. And, like the German and Russian dictators, it continued, the Ayatollah's potential for shaping events in a crucial part of the world went well beyond the present crisis that he had fomented. Such sweet reason did not, however, ameliorate the subscribers' outrage over Khomeini's selection. "Even Jane Fonda would have been an improvement," one reader fumed. "Is this responsible journalism?" asked another, while yet a third claimed that the Ayatollah's Man of the Year portrait would be taken as a visual proof among Iranians that their leader was winning "his war of wills with the American people."[1]

In some quarters at *TIME* itself, antipathy for the magazine's 1979 Man of the Year apparently also ran deep. Shortly after Brad Holland's original Man of the Year rendering of the Ayatollah was hung in an office there, it disappeared and was found later languishing in a toilet stall, where it had been rather unceremoniously deposited.

1. *TIME*, January 7, 1980, p. 3; January 21, 1980, p. 10.

Man of the Year 1980
Ronald Reagan (born 1911)

Aaron Shikler (born 1922)

Essence of oil on paper, 66 x 45.5 cm. (26 x 17 7/8 in.), 1980
National Portrait Gallery, Smithsonian Institution; gift of Time, Inc.
NPG.84.TC140

TIME awarded its 1980 Man of the Year honors to Ronald Reagan partly because he had just claimed the White House in the recent November elections. Equally significant, however, was the fact that the President-elect's strong conservatism seemed to be signaling a marked shift in America's political climate and that, in his calls for such things as reduced Federal involvement in welfare and business, he was ushering in an era that would be quite different from recent presidential administrations—Republican and Democratic alike. Or, as *TIME* put it, Reagan was not only the Man of the Year; he was also the "idea of the year."[1]

For the making of Reagan's Man of the Year likeness, *TIME* enlisted the services of Aaron Shikler, who had attracted nationwide attention in 1971 with the unveiling of his official White House portraits of John F. Kennedy and his widow, Jacqueline Onassis. Among the traits characterizing Shikler's portrait style is a sense of momentary intimacy that he achieves largely through sensitive lighting and unconventional poses. That quality is abundantly apparent in his depiction of Reagan.

In attempting to summarize Reagan's leadership style, *TIME* noted that he did not attempt to dominate people around him but rather beguiled them with his good nature, low-keyed voice, and home-grown sense of humor. To a large extent, it was this down-to-earth openness that artist Aaron Shikler seems to have wanted to capture in Reagan's portrait.

For his sittings with Reagan, Shikler had to go to California where, closeted at his ranch, his subject was in the process of selecting a Cabinet. When the artist drew up in a hired chauffeured limousine, the reporters gathered at the President-elect's retreat immediately assumed that Shikler's mode of transportation meant that he must be a potential member of that body arriving for consultation. After it became clear who he was, some members of the press corps began putting two and two together, and this became one instance where *TIME* failed in its attempt to keep its Man of the Year choice a secret.

1. *TIME*, January 5, 1981, p. 12.

Men of the Year 1983
Ronald Reagan (born 1911)
Yuri Andropov (1914–1984)

Through much of 1983, the news had been dominated by an increasingly hostile situation between the United States and the Soviet Union. With the breakup of disarmament talks between these two superpowers, the proliferation of more Soviet and American missiles in Europe, and the Russians' downing of a civilian South Korean plane venturing into their airspace, it seemed by year's end that the international détente of recent years was over and that the second cold war was begun. As *TIME* saw it, the two individuals most central in this unsettling turn of events were American President Ronald Reagan and his Soviet counterpart, Yuri Andropov. Accordingly, on January 2, 1984, grimly standing back-to-back as if ready for a pistol duel, these two world leaders found themselves on *TIME*'s cover, sharing the magazine's Man of the Year title.

The artist charged with making this double image was Alfred Leslie, well known for a startlingly direct delineation of his subjects that often gives his pictures a chilling quality. This sharpness of style made Leslie an unusually happy choice for pictorializing the central thrust of *TIME*'s Man of the Year article. To achieve his desired effects, however, Leslie generally insisted on doing his portraits from life sittings, and unfortunately that was not possible in this case. Instead, he was forced to rely on a combination of photographs and models who resembled Reagan and Andropov and were clothed in suits similar in cut and style to what they normally wore. Despite this secondhand approach to the work, Leslie succeeded in creating an image that was almost overwhelming in its icy realism.

Alfred Leslie (born 1927)

Oil on canvas, 152.4 x 137.2 cm. (60 x 54 in.), 1983
National Portrait Gallery, Smithsonian Institution; gift of Time, Inc.
NPG.86.TC33

Woman of the Year 1986
Corazon Aquino (born 1933)

Diana Walker (born 1942)

Color photograph, 1986
Courtesy of Time, Inc.

When Filipino President Corazon Aquino became *TIME*'s 1986 Woman of the Year, she was by no means the first member of her sex to claim that distinction. Fifty years earlier the future Duchess of Windsor, Wallis Simpson, whose affair with England's Edward VIII had made headlines through much of 1936, had taken the honor. In 1952 Elizabeth II's accession to Britain's throne once again inspired *TIME* to change its Man of the Year title to Woman of the Year, and in 1975 the increasing prominence of females in American public life led the magazine to designate eleven noted members of the fair sex as its Women of the Year. But, although Aquino was not the first Woman of the Year, in certain respects she was significantly different from these newsmaking predecessors. For *TIME* had placed Aquino on its most important cover not because a king had courted her, or because she had inherited a throne that made her the politically powerless emblem of a great nation, or because she was part of a noteworthy collective phenomenon. Rather she found herself there for much the same reason that most of her Man of the Year counterparts had in the past. Simply put, Aquino had become Woman of the Year because like a de Gaulle, an Eisenhower, or a Khrushchev, she was in the full sense a political leader of the world, who in her own right had accomplished much in twelve months and might perhaps achieve yet more.

The maker of Aquino's Woman of the Year likeness, Diana Walker, spent more than ten days in the Philippines photographing Aquino for *TIME*. Despite the press of public business, Aquino proved an unusually agreeable subject, and she readily acquiesced to Walker's suggestion that she pose for her cover image dressed in red. In the final picture, Walker sought to capture the "deep serenity" and "self-possession" that she came to regard as Aquino's most remarkable strengths. In an attempt to underscore those qualities pictorially, she asked Aquino to pose against a simple, dark background that turned out to be a mahogany door found in the Philippine President's office.[1]

1. Conversation between the author and
Diana Walker, March 1987.

Checklist of *TIME*
Man of the Year covers

1927
 Charles Lindbergh 1902–1974
  Aviator

Samuel Johnson Woolf (1880–1948)
Charcoal on paper, 1927
Germantown Friends School,
 Philadelphia, Pennsylvania

1928
 Walter P. Chrysler 1875–1940
  American car magnate

Samuel Johnson Woolf (1880–1948)
Painting
Unlocated

1929
 Owen D. Young 1874–1962
  Formulator of revised German
  reparations agreement, 1929

David Cleeland (lifedates unknown)
Painting
Unlocated

1930
 Mohandas Karamchand (Mahatma)
  Gandhi 1869–1948
  Leader of India's independence
  movement

Vladimir Perlilieff (lifedates
 unknown)
Painting
Unlocated

1931
 Pierre Laval 1883–1945
  French Premier

Harris Rodvogin (lifedates unknown)
Painting
Unlocated

1932
 Franklin D. Roosevelt 1882–1945
  American President-elect

O. J. Jordan (lifedates unknown)
Color photograph
Unlocated

1933
 Hugh S. Johnson 1882–1942
  Chief of America's National
  Recovery Administration

O. J. Jordan (lifedates unknown)
Color photograph
Unlocated

1934
 Franklin D. Roosevelt 1882–1945
  American President

Keystone Photographs (active 1892–
 circa 1939)
Black-and-white photograph
Unlocated

1935
 Haile Selassie (born Tefarrie Makonnen)
  1892–1975
  Ethiopian Emperor

Jerry Farnsworth (1895–1982)
Painting
Unlocated

1936
 Wallis Warfield Simpson (Duchess of
  Windsor) 1896–1986
  American socialite

Dorothy Wilding (lifedates unknown)
Painting
Unlocated

1937
 General Chiang Kai-shek 1887–1975
 Madame Chiang Kai-shek born 1898?
  Chinese leaders

Samuel Johnson Woolf (1880–1948)
Oil on canvas, 1937
National Portrait Gallery,
 Smithsonian Institution; gift of the
 estate of Muriel Woolf Hobson

1938
  Adolf Hitler 1889–1945
    German dictator

  Rudolph Charles von Ripper (1905–1960)
  Etching, 1938
  Prints Collection, The New York Public Library

1939
  Joseph Stalin 1879–1953
    Soviet dictator

  Ernest Hamlin Baker (1889–1975)
  Painting
  Unlocated

1940
  Winston Churchill 1874–1965
    British Prime Minister

  Unidentified artist
  Painting
  Unlocated

1941
  Franklin D. Roosevelt 1882–1945
    American President

  Ernest Hamlin Baker (1889–1975)
  Watercolor on paper, 1941
  Harry Ransom Humanities Research Center, The University of Texas at Austin, Iconography Collection

1942
  Joseph Stalin 1879–1953
    Soviet dictator

  Boris Artzybasheff (1899–1965)
  Gouache on board, 1942
  Syracuse University Art Collections

1943
  George C. Marshall 1880–1959
    American military chief of staff

  Ernest Hamlin Baker (1889–1975)
  Painting
  Unlocated

1944
  Dwight D. Eisenhower 1890–1969
    American general

  Ernest Hamlin Baker (1889–1975)
  Painting
  Unlocated

1945
  Harry S Truman 1884–1972
    American President

  Boris Artzybasheff (1899–1965)
  Painting
  Unlocated

1946
  James F. Byrnes 1879–1972
    American secretary of state

  Boris Chaliapin (1904–1979)
  Painting
  Unlocated

1947
  George C. Marshall 1880–1959
    American secretary of state

  Ernest Hamlin Baker (1889–1975)
  Watercolor on board, 1947
  George C. Marshall Research Foundation, Lexington, Virginia

1948
  Harry S Truman 1884–1972
    American President

  Ernest Hamlin Baker (1889–1975)
  Painting
  Unlocated

1949
  Winston Churchill 1874–1965
    British statesman (Man of the Half-Century)

  Ernest Hamlin Baker (1889–1975)
  Watercolor on board, 1949
  National Portrait Gallery, Smithsonian Institution; gift of Time, Inc.

1950
   G.I. Joe
      American soldier (*TIME*'s first
      collective Man of the Year)

   Ernest Hamlin Baker (1889–1975)
   Painting
   Unlocated

1951
   Mohammed Mossadegh circa 1880–1967
      Iranian Leader

   Boris Chaliapin (1904–1979)
   Painting
   Unlocated

1952
   Queen Elizabeth II born 1926
      English monarch

   Boris Chaliapin (1904–1979)
   Painting
   Unlocated

1953
   Konrad Adenauer 1876–1967
      West German Chancellor

   Boris Artzybasheff (1899–1965)
   Painting
   Unlocated

1954
   John Foster Dulles 1888–1959
      American secretary of state

   Ernest Hamlin Baker (1889–1975)
   Painting
   Unlocated

1955
   Harlow H. Curtice 1893–1962
      American car magnate

   Boris Artzybasheff (1899–1965)
   Painting
   Unlocated

1956
   "Hungarian Patriot"

   Boris Chaliapin (1904–1979)
   Painting
   Unlocated

1957
   Nikita Khrushchev 1884–1971
      Soviet leader

   Boris Artzybasheff (1899–1965)
   Tempera and polymer on masonite,
   1957
   National Portrait Gallery,
   Smithsonian Institution; gift of
   Time, Inc.

1958
   Charles de Gaulle 1890–1970
      French President

   Bernard Buffet (born 1928)
   Oil on canvas, 1958
   National Portrait Gallery,
   Smithsonian Institution; gift of
   Time, Inc.

1959
   Dwight D. Eisenhower 1890–1969
      American President

   Bernard Safran (born 1924)
   Oil on masonite, 1959
   National Portrait Gallery,
   Smithsonian Institution; gift of
   Time, Inc.

1960
   "American Scientists"
   George Beadle born 1903
      Biologist
   John Enders 1897–1985
      Bacteriologist
   Charles Draper 1901–1987
      Aeronautical engineer
   Donald Glaser born 1926
      Physicist
   Joshua Lederberg born 1925
      Biologist
   William Libby born 1908
      Chemist

Linus Pauling born 1901
   Chemist
Edward Purcell born 1912
   Physicist
Emilio Segrè born 1905
   Physicist
William Shockley born 1910
   Physicist
Edward Teller born 1908
   Physicist
Charles Townes born 1915
   Physicist
James Van Allen born 1914
   Physicist
Robert B. Woodward born 1917
   Chemist

Unidentified photographers
Color photographs
Unlocated

1961
   John F. Kennedy 1917–1963
      American President

   Pietro Annigoni (born 1910)
   Watercolor on paper, 1961
   National Portrait Gallery,
      Smithsonian Institution; gift of
      Time, Inc.

1962
   Pope John XXIII 1881–1963
      Leader of the Catholic Church

   Bernard Safran (born 1924)
   Oil on masonite, 1962
   National Portrait Gallery,
      Smithsonian Institution; gift of
      Time, Inc.

1963
   Martin Luther King, Jr. 1929–1968
      American civil rights leader

   Robert Vickrey (born 1926)
   Tempera on paper, 1963
   National Portrait Gallery,
      Smithsonian Institution; gift of
      Time, Inc.

1964
   Lyndon B. Johnson 1908–1973
      American President

   Peter Hurd (1904–1984) and
      Henriette Wyeth (born 1907)
   Tempera on paper, 1964
   National Portrait Gallery,
      Smithsonian Institution; gift of
      Time, Inc.

1965
   William Westmoreland born 1914
      American general

   Robert Berks (born 1922)
   Clay, 1965
   Presented to sitter

1966
   "Twenty-Five and Under"
      Americans under the age of
      twenty-five

   Robert Vickrey (born 1926)
   Tempera and ink on board, 1966
   National Portrait Gallery,
      Smithsonian Institution; gift of
      Time, Inc.

1967
   Lyndon B. Johnson 1908–1973
      American President

   David Levine (born 1926)
   Pen and ink on board, 1967
   National Portrait Gallery,
      Smithsonian Institution; gift of
      Time, Inc.

1968
   "Astronauts"
   William Anders born 1933
   Frank Borman born 1928
   James Lovell born 1928
      First humans to circle the moon

   Hector Garrido (born 1927)
   Acrylic and tempera on masonite,
      1968
   National Portrait Gallery,
      Smithsonian Institution; gift of
      Time, Inc.

1969
"The Middle Americans"
   Tradition-minded Americans

Vin Giuliani (1930–1976)
Metal, wood, and paper collage, 1969
National Portrait Gallery,
   Smithsonian Institution; gift of
   Time, Inc.

1970
Willy Brandt born 1913
   West German Chancellor

George Giusti (born 1908)
Aluminum, steel, and colored paper,
   1970
National Portrait Gallery,
   Smithsonian Institution; gift of
   Time, Inc.

1971
Richard M. Nixon born 1913
   American President

Stanley Glaubach (1925–1973)
Papier-mâché, 1971
National Portrait Gallery,
   Smithsonian Institution; gift of
   Time, Inc.

1972
Richard Nixon born 1913
   American President
Henry Kissinger born 1923
   Head of the National Security
   Council

Marisol (Escobar) (born 1930)
Marble, 1972
National Portrait Gallery,
   Smithsonian Institution; gift of
   Time, Inc.

1973
John J. Sirica born 1904
   Federal judge

Stanislaw Zagorski (born 1933)
Acrylic, metallic paint, and cloth on
   board, 1973
National Portrait Gallery,
   Smithsonian Institution; gift of
   Time, Inc.

1974
Faisal ibn Abdul Aziz al Saud 1906?–
   1975
   Saudi Arabian King

Robert Peak (born 1928)
Painting
Presented to Saudi Arabia

1975
"American Women"
Susan Brownmiller born 1935
   Writer
Kathleen Byerly born 1945
   Naval officer
Alison Cheek born 1928
   Episcopal cleric
Jill Conway born 1934
   College president
Elizabeth (Betty) Ford born 1918
   First lady
Ella Grasso 1919–1981
   State governor
Carla Hills born 1934
   Secretary of Housing and Urban
   Development
Barbara Jordan born 1936
   Congresswoman
Billie Jean King born 1943
   Athlete
Susie M. Sharp born 1907
   State supreme court chief justice
Carol Sutton born 1932
   Newspaper editor
Addie Wyatt born 1924
   Labor leader

Unidentified photographers
Color photographs
Unlocated

1976
James Earl (Jimmy) Carter, Jr. born
   1924
   American President-elect

James Wyeth (born 1946)
Watercolor on paper, 1976
National Portrait Gallery,
   Smithsonian Institution; gift of
   Time, Inc.

1977
  Anwar Sadat 1918–1981
    Egyptian President

  Audrey Flack (born 1931)
  Painting, 1977
  Presented to sitter

1978
  Teng Hsiao-p'ing born 1904?
    Chinese Vice-Premier

  Richard Hess (born 1934)
  Oil on canvas, 1978
  National Portrait Gallery,
    Smithsonian Institution; gift of
    Time, Inc.

1979
  Ayatollah Ruhollah Khomeini born 1900
    Iranian Leader

  Brad Holland (born 1944)
  Oil on canvas, 1979
  National Portrait Gallery,
    Smithsonian Institution; gift of
    Time, Inc.

1980
  Ronald Reagan born 1911
    American President-elect

  Aaron Shikler (born 1922)
  Essence of oil on paper, 1980
  National Portrait Gallery,
    Smithsonian Institution; gift of
    Time, Inc.

1981
  Lech Walesa born 1943
    Polish labor leader

  James Dine (born 1935)
  Charcoal, graphite, watercolor, and
    chalk on paper with photographs
  National Portrait Gallery,
    Smithsonian Institution; gift of
    Time, Inc.

1982
  "The Computer Moves In"
    The computer

  George Segal (born 1924)
  Plaster figures in domestic setting
  Time, Inc.

1983
  Ronald Reagan born 1911
    American President
  Yuri Andropov 1914–1984
    Soviet Union's General Secretary
    of the Communist party

  Alfred Leslie (born 1927)
  Oil on canvas, 1983
  National Portrait Gallery,
    Smithsonian Institution; gift of
    Time, Inc.

1984
  Peter Uberroth born 1937
    Organizer of U.S. Olympics

  Paul Davis (born 1938)
  Acrylic and collage on illustration
    board
  Time, Inc.

1985
  Deng Xiaoping born 1904
    Chairman of the Chinese
    Communist party

  Robert Rauschenberg (born 1925)
  Multimedia collage, 1985
  Time, Inc.

1986
  Corazon Aquino born 1933
    Filipino President

  Diana Walker (born 1942)
  Color photograph, 1986
  Time, Inc.

Selected Readings

Elson, Robert T. *Time Inc.: The Intimate History of a Publishing Enterprise, 1923–1941*. Vol. 1. New York, 1968.

———. *The World of Time Inc.: The Intimate History of a Publishing Enterprise, 1941–1960*. Vol. 2. New York, 1973.

Hoopes, Roy. *Ralph Ingersoll*. New York, 1985.

Prendergast, Curtis, and Geoffrey Colvin. *The World of Time Inc.: The Intimate History of a Changing Enterprise, 1960–1980*. Vol. 3. New York, 1986.

Swanberg, William A. *Luce and His Empire*. New York, 1972.

This book was composed by Monotype Composition, Inc. of Baltimore, Maryland, on a Linotron 202. The text and display faces are both Janson. The original version of Janson was cut in the seventeenth century by Nicholas Kis in Amsterdam and was redesigned by C.H. Griffith for Mergenthaler Linotype in 1937. The book was printed on Warren's eighty pound Lustro Offset Enamel Dull stock by Collins Lithographing and Printing Company, Inc., of Baltimore, Maryland. It was designed by Linda McKnight, of the Smithsonian Institution Press, Washington, D.C.